RETARD

RETARD

DIANE O'REILLY

Glenbridge Publishing Ltd.
1989

Lines on page 144, 145 and 147 from "Everything is Beautiful," words and music by Ray Stevens, Copyright © 1970, Ahab Music Company, Inc.

While a few of the essential events and experiences recounted in this book occurred in more than one year and in more than one place, they are all fundamentally true and have been compressed for the benefit of the reader.

The characters in this book are based on real people. Names and details have been changed to ensure privacy.

Copyright © 1989 by Diane O'Reilly

All rights reserved. Except for brief quotations in critical articles or reviews, this book, or parts thereof, may not be reproduced in any form without permission in writing from the publisher. For further information contact Glenbridge Publishing Ltd., Macomb, Illinois, 61455.

Library of Congress Catalog Card Number: 88-83478
International Standard Book Number: 0 944435-05-X

To my three children
and
To my annex children

Contents

Foreword ix

Introduction 1

I.   Unknown Territory 3

II.   A Real Beginning 19

III. Unnecessary Handicaps 40

IV. Two Steps Forward 54

V.   One Step Back 70

VI. Successes Great and Small 82

VII. Out in the Real World 99

VIII. Holiday Rewards 111

IX. Spring Creeps In 129

X.   Signs of Growth 144

XI. Laws for the Education
      of the Handicapped 159

XII. Parental Aid 171

Epilogue 185

Bibliography 191

FOREWORD

We live in a society that appears in many ways to value differences or exceptionalities. Conversations with parents whose children are the best readers in their classes or the best gymnasts on their teams reveal proud supportive parents. When differences, however, move in a direction that we have designated as less competent, pride is often replaced with shame and embarrassment. The children you will meet in this book were placed in a special class because they were different in ways that were not viewed as positive by their teachers and other school officials. They may not have been able to "keep up" with their peers in completing school work. Some behaved differently socially or emotionally. Some were either too aggressive or not aggressive enough.

This book is about children. The children were labeled educationally mentally retarded. It is about a sensitive, caring, and competent teacher, about teachers who appear to hold low and negative expectations for the children, and about the relationships that develop between children and their teachers, about a school system and a society that is trying to help these children, but in the process of "helping" raise questions about the degree to which they value these differences. Finally, the book is about the children's environments, especially their school classroom. Other environments include inner city homes and gang-dominated streets.

You are invited to "sit in" on the children's class for a school year. You will learn to know the children and their teacher, and will follow the progress of the children as they learn to trust their teacher.

The initial days in the class provide examples of many of the problems associated with special classes—low or nonexistent expectations for the children, an environment dominated by punitive teacher-child interactions, and low self-esteem on the part of the children and class. One of the most interesting opportunities afforded the reader is the opportunity to observe how the class is transformed from an unhappy, disruptive, and unproductive place to a positive learning environment. The teacher began the transformation by treating each student with respect and dignity. She offered consistent examples of respect and valuing of the children. At the same time, the class became a laboratory in which conflicts and values were negotiated. As respect for the value of each person was demonstrated and learned, competing strategies of intimidation and power were avoided.

Children in the class were immediately given important work to do. They were evaluated to determine their reading levels and were assigned work consistent with their previous learning and knowledge. Once the teacher was assured that work assigned to students was within the range of work they were capable of doing, she was able to communicate positive and firm expectations for its completion.

The teacher recognized the social learning needs of the students. Although completing school work was given high priority in the class, learning how to live with other persons was an equally important objective. The consistent statement and enforcement of rules that guided the way students related to each other and the commitment to encouraging the students to explore, discuss, and value these rules were major teaching techniques used. As the children learned to negotiate social exchange, they were able to work together cooperatively and to encourage and support their mutual progress.

For some of the children school was perhaps the most stable and secure part of their lives. The teacher recognized the effects of the negative experiences outside of school but was not immobilized by them. In one case she tried to change these conditions through a home visit to improve a child's attendance. But for the most part she listened to the children and affirmed their value and ability to succeed within the circumstances of the classroom.

As a consequence of the teacher's efforts, many of the children learned to read, to live more positively and peacefully with each other, and perhaps most significantly, to believe they were important and valued persons.

As we observe the learning of the children, it is important that we not ignore the teacher's learning. While we are observing an excellent teacher, we are also observing the struggle with reconciling middle class values of hard work, self discipline, and social competence with the quite different values of the children. There are many examples of situations in which these conflicts are clearly illustrated. In each case the teacher is able to negotiate her value conflicts in a way that does not demean or devalue the student. The teacher's actions are mediated by a powerful underlying respect for the dignity and potential of each student. As each conflict arises, be it a threat to kill another student or a failure to wipe a runny nose, the personal value of each student is evident in the teacher's response.

Some of the most difficult conflicts are not with the children but with other individuals in the children's environment. Clear examples are those in which other teachers fail to recognize the dignity and potential of the children, or "system" constraints, when test results negatively affect the lives of the children. The children also would make devaluing comments and actions toward each other.

Along with the pragmatic competence for teaching these children and the knowledge that they were learning, the teacher also wonders if all the children need to be in the class and if there might not be a better way to meet their needs. The class described in this book represents an early attempt to provide educational opportunities for children who have difficulty learning in the "regular" system. The teacher raises a number of important questions about her work. Questions such as: Are all of these children really "retarded"? Could they have been taught in "regular" classes? Were test results used to place the children in the class accurate? To what extent were self-confidence, self-esteem and emotional, cultural, and environmental factors, rather than intellectual factors, related to the children's school difficulties? Each of these questions has been raised recently by professionals in the field.

One of the realities of providing programs like special education classes for children appears to be that in the process of attempting to help them we inadvertently may hurt them in other ways. Our help may have side effects that appear to be reduced expectations on the part of teachers, parents, and the students themselves. There can be limitations of opportunities for "special" students to learn from positive models, and the increase in social distance between "special" and "normal" people. The reader is encouraged to consider the effects of the special class on each of the children and to reach his or her own conclusion.

Charles Galloway, writing about the social context in which we make decisions about people who are different, urges us to consider two guidelines when planning services for persons who are different. The first guideline he calls the developmental assumption. Simply stated, this assumption holds that all individuals, regardless of their assigned labels or level of disability are capable of continuous development. Educationally, it means that for each student there is a "next thing to learn" and the task of the teacher is to identify that step and help the child learn it. One of the outstanding strengths of the teacher you will meet is her commitment to this assumption.

The second assumption presented by Galloway states that society is responsible for equitable allocation of resources, and that assurance of development requires more resources for some people than for others. For these children, the allocation of resources question includes the question of in what setting the resources should be provided. Each of these children will take more of the teacher's time than children who have no difficulty learning. Should another teacher be provided for a special class or could a teacher's aide be hired for a regular class? Or might a reduction in class size offer the additional time needed so the children could be taught together with non-handicapped children. The allocation of resources question is one that is addressed with difficulty in our society. Observations of classrooms suggest that children who have difficulty learning do receive attention from their teachers. Unfortunately, it is too often attention that is negative in nature and may add nothing to the child's development or learning status. In a longer time frame it is important to consider the possibility that if sufficient resources are not committed to teaching children in such a way that the developmental assumption is met, society may allocate resources to the individual in other forms, such as unemployment payments, hospital, law enforcement, and prison costs. One must consider the possibility of a "pay me now or pay me later" component to this decision.

We often make the assumption that when people are identified as retarded they are very much alike. The perceptive reader will note that among the class of children identified as retarded there were very significant individual differences. The lesson that may be learned from this observation is important. Children need to be considered as individuals. The label that is attached to them tells us little about their characteristics or their potential. Each of the children in the classroom responded in varying ways and in varying degrees to a teacher who treated them as individuals who had common needs for love, respect, and good teaching.

Hal Hiebert, Ed.D.
Department of Psychology-Special Education
University of Wisconsin, La Crosse

Acknowledgments

For their advice and assistance, I wish to thank Sharon O'Reilly, Maureen Howard, Burley Howard, John Sarnowski, and Pamela D. Burdett, M.L.S., Stetson University College of Law Library.

The encouragement and comments of Hal Hiebert, Ed.D., Mary Irene Zotti, Kay Guncheon, Marjerry Geyer, Sharlene Sakol, and Frank O'Reilly, who generously gave their time to read the manuscript, were invaluable to me.

My especial appreciation goes to the children who inspired this book by being the individuals they are.

Finally, I am grateful to James A. Keene, my editor, for his suggestions and careful editing.

Introduction

This story, about school children who were labeled "mentally handicapped," was written in an effort to help broaden understanding for all exceptional children. Perhaps their story will help bring to those who teach or who are associated with similar children a greater awareness of their needs and capabilities.

The children were shoved aside by the educational system. They were rejected by their peers and sometimes by their families. They rejected each other. They even rejected themselves.

The children's problems that could be seen were serious; their unseen problems were often devastating. Many of the problems and the resulting failures that robbed the children of positive self-images need never have occurred.

Some of the children in this book grew up to make a contribution to our society; each of them had the potential to do so.

I

UNKNOWN TERRITORY

Harvey walked into the classroom on his hands, flipped to his feet and gave me a "top this" smile. He was a slim, winsome, eight-year-old black boy, about the size of a five-year-old. He had introduced himself to me before school by shinning himself up to the ground floor window of our classroom. He had held onto the windowsill and used the crevasses between the bricks for toe holds. He wanted to be sure that he was noticed. Indeed, he was.

Head bowed, a pale girl with limp hair, the color of weak tea, slipped through the door after him. She was so quiet and self-effacing that the air hardly moved as she passed by me.

There was a rustling sound outside the door. Sam bounded in, gave both the girl and Harvey a shove, turned and slammed the door. He grabbed the knob with both hands and used his body weight to hold the door shut.

Apprehensive faces stared through the window in the door.

I put my hands on Sam's shoulders to move him aside. At my touch, he whirled to face me and hunched down protectively. Did he expect some violent action from a teacher, one who was not much bigger than he was at that?

When I opened the door, the children detoured both Sam and me. They went quickly to the desks that had their names printed on tagboard taped to them.

The last to enter was Fred. Instead of sitting at his desk, he folded his angular body under it and pulled his chair securely in behind him; his head protruded once, then withdrew, like a turtle into his shell.

Sam didn't respond when I asked him to go to his desk in the rear of the room so we did a stately minuet. As I advanced a step, he retreated a step. There was no music with this dance, however. He finally bumped into his chair and sat down.

This was a primary Educable Mentally Handicapped (EMH) classroom in the annex of a main school that was three blocks away. The annex consisted of six classrooms and a gymnasium, all on the ground level.

The classroom windows faced a wide avenue. Across the avenue, four vintage houses bolstered each other up, standing aloof from the adjoining vacant lots where wrecking crews had done their work. Decades of decline meant that wrecking crews were now a familiar sight in this neighborhood. Bleak window eyes in the remaining houses stared back at us. Trash blew along the avenue that separated us.

It was a Wednesday in mid-October. I had just returned from a leave of absence and I had been assigned this class. I had taught first grade in the main school until the previous year, when I was needed at home.

My briefing for this class had consisted of a description of Sam's problems with the law and society in general. He had been caught breaking into the school annex at night and, on another occasion, breaking into a neighbor's apartment with two older boys. He was suspected of being involved in many other break-ins and was reputed to be an intolerable bully with younger or weaker children.

Sam had passed his tenth birthday and was over the age limit for a primary EMH class. He was almost eleven. The intermediate Educable Mentally Handicapped class, to which the students progressed after primary EMH, had reached its quota of fifteen children, so Sam had remained in this classroom. He was scheduled to be transferred to a special school for boys who were disciplinary problems; however, the transfer had not come through yet.

This class had had a different substitute teacher almost every day since the beginning of the school year. On some days, when no substitute was available, the children had been divided up and sent to the other five classrooms in the annex. The most determined substitute had lasted only three days. One substitute had given up in the middle of her first day.

The class, with all of its inherent problems, had slipped through a crack in the educational system. Their previous assigned teacher was eligible to retire. After attending the first few days of school, she had gone on sick leave. By using her sick leave days, accumulated over many years, she could be paid for all school holidays as well as the sick days. When the sick days were used up, she would formally retire.

Because the class already had an assigned teacher, I was considered a full-time substitute rather than an assigned teacher. But since it was the only class available, and I had taught in the main school and knew many of the younger children and some of their siblings, I preferred teaching here to starting again in a new school.

Of course, the class would have been much better off had the assigned teacher been able to retire and still be paid for the additional time. It then would have had a chance of having a regularly assigned teacher at the beginning of the school year; that is, if one could be found to take it.

The school neighborhood was one of the least desirable in the city. Some of the once fashionable homes, all of which had been divided up into apartments, had been torn down, and many of those that did still stand were unfit to inhabit. In addition, most rents were exorbitant. Consequently some of the families moved frequently, trying to find decent homes for reasonable rent, but causing their children to interrupt their education by changing schools much too often.

Also, the need of the mentally handicapped children for frequent repetition of material, and the low frustration level of some of the students makes teaching these classes especially difficult for substitutes and certified teachers alike. Almost all teachers, given a choice, select the regular classroom in which to teach.

After having had six weeks of constant change, any class would have been difficult to settle down, and mentally handicapped children usually have more difficulty adjusting to change than other children. The class was quite a challenge, but I was anxious to return to teaching, and the sun shining in the many windows was encouraging.

There was a seating chart on my desk, for which I was grateful. As I picked it up, Sam rushed forward and grabbed a marble that a tall boy near the front of the room was rolling back and forth across his desk. The boy's name was Johnny, according to the seating chart. Johnny looked bewildered and made no attempt to get the marble back.

"Sam, give the marble back," I said sternly. This brought a laugh from Sam as he lunged for the back of the room. He managed to elbow a small girl en route. The little girl didn't make a sound. Her body was rigid; she held her eyes open wide, alert for signs of more trouble.

"Fine. Stay where you are." I pushed Sam's desk further back, almost to the corner, where he faced me defiantly. "You can stay at this desk until you are ready to give me the marble and go to work with the rest of the class."

I pushed his chair to him and brought two more chairs to his side of the room, placing myself on one of them, between him and the rest of the class. The other children had been quiet during the confrontation, but now a muttering sound came from Debra, a small girl in a front corner of the room. A low buzz began in other parts of the room.

Sheila shrieked, "Debra said something nasty to me."

Harvey ground a pencil in the pencil sharpener. Nellie, a heavy, pear-shaped girl with thin blonde hair, rocked and hummed to herself at her desk behind Harvey's. Meanwhile, Fred crouched under his desk and whispered to his fingers, which he wiggled in front of his face.

Although Sam, the chief agitator, was now held at bay, the classroom was bedlam, and I was the caretaker. It was certainly not a learning atmosphere. I had had more than twice the number of students in this classroom in previous regular classes, at times, but this class seemed larger, making up in sound and disorder for the smaller number of students.

As I looked around the classroom, I noticed a boy named Norman. He was also looking around. He had a peculiar expression on his face. I thought I recognized that expression. He looked around as if he wondered where he was and how he got there.

There obviously would be no class introduction from me today. The children would have to be given some work immediately for there to be any order in the class. The most important thing I needed was some quiet time with them to determine their capabilities.

Since he seemed more energetic than the rest, Harvey was put in charge of handing out drawing paper. The children were told to draw themselves and their families, a task they had probably been asked to do many times over since the beginning of the school year. They were to put their names in the upper right-hand corner of the paper, if they were capable of it, so that their work could be identified. I was reluctant to leave my precarious control over Sam to go to the front of the room and write the school name and the date on the chalkboard for the children to copy.

While the others drew, I asked those children whom I called to bring their reading book over and read it to me. Debra was the first one I called. Her eyebrows were drawn down to the bridge of her nose in a scowl, and one fat pigtail stood straight out on each side of her triangular face. Her fierce expression didn't slacken as she read part of a story in a primer. She read quickly and accurately. She was obviously capable of more difficult material.

"Debra, you read perfectly. You will certainly have a harder reading book soon." My remarks and smile only drew a look of disgust and a *sotto voce* comment from her as she mumbled her way back to her desk. I thought I heard the word "honky."

Nora, the shy girl who had followed Harvey into the classroom, was the next to read. Her clothes were as soiled and neglected as her hair. Her forlorn appearance was increased by her half-hemmed, half-unhemmed dress. She brought the same primer Debra had brought with her. She read it accurately, but slowly, in a faltering voice that seemed to expect correction momentarily. She never looked up. My praise and the suggestion that she, too, might earn a new book soon brought a slight smile, but her side glance that never met mine, seemed to question whether or not I would be there later. Perhaps other teachers before me had promised the children new books.

William, who sat behind Nora, was next. His appearance in this classroom had shocked me, but Sam had left me no time to greet William.

This handsome black boy with large expressive eyes had been in my first grade class two years before, but he had been absent constantly. Frequent calls to his mother had not increased his spasmodic attendance at school. He had been immature, and seemingly spoiled, but he had not seemed mentally handicapped. He had transferred to another school in March of his first grade year. Now he had transferred back to this school. He brought the same primer he had had when I last saw him. At least he could read it well and be assured that he, too, could have a new book soon.

Norman, whose expression was that of an alien in a strange land wondering how he got there, was next. He read the primer competently. His deportment was serious, like an elderly gentleman, brooking no interruptions and inviting no questions or familiarities.

Sheila, a tall black girl with a scar like a gnarled root extending from her temple to the corner of her mouth, shrieked as if in alarm when I called her name. She, too, brought the same primer and read it adequately but with a noticeable lack of interest.

Harvey, Johnny, Annabelle, and Kevin read haltingly in the same book. They looked up frequently, as if expecting me to correct them. It was painfully apparent that they were not confident of their ability to read. Harvey had great difficulty keeping his place on the page. None of them read as well as the first four had.

All the children had the same book. Apparently no teacher had stayed long enough to discover the reading level of each student. Several of the children obviously knew the primer vocabulary well and should have had more challenging material by now.

Nellie and even Verna, who at six years of age was the youngest child in the room and who was Annabelle's little sister, had this same primer. Neither could read it, although Nellie remembered the names of the boy and the girl in the pictures. When I asked Fred to come up, the class, in unison, assured me that Fred stayed under his desk "lotsa time." He didn't look up when I spoke to him, but I could feel his anxiety as he waited for me to turn my attention elsewhere and forget him. I felt sure that the same primer was in his desk.

Sam either couldn't read or was determined not to read for me. My request for him to bring his book over and read was met with a muttered "nah." My physical presence next to him had restricted his movements to jiggling and desk scraping. He had done no work, but I had gained the time to tentatively identify the reading ability of most of the children.

Unfortunately, it had taken too long for me to check their reading, and I had delayed their "toilet recess" until it was too late. Little Verna began to cry as her bladder emptied on the floor. Her big sister Annabelle, apparently accustomed to taking charge of her in such situations, went to a cupboard, got out the paper towels, and hurriedly began to blot up the tattletale puddle.

While the other children lined up for the delayed trip to the washroom, I stood with my hand outstretched in front of Sam, waiting for him to give me the marble. Finally, the desire to get out of the room won, and he grudgingly gave me the prize, which I foolishly returned to Johnny.

The ritual of handing out towels and soap was performed. We made an erratic procession to the girls' washroom, with

Debra leading and with me in the rear next to Sam.

The girls went into their washroom first, while I waited in the hallway with the boys. When the girls came out, they waited in line with me while the boys went into their washroom. Almost immediately, a pained cry sent me in after them. Six brown and one white very startled faces looked up as their teacher for the day entered the boys' washroom.

Sam had managed to get Johnny down on the floor where he was straddling him, trying to get the marble out of his pants pocket. Johnny was a husky boy for an eight-year-old and almost as tall as Sam, but he lacked the coordination of the older boy and certainly lacked confidence in his ability to protect himself from Sam.

Since he ignored my request to get up, I pulled Sam off Johnny. Johnny's pocket was torn, and he was close to tears. The other boys huddled nervously against the farthest wall. Sam moved away from me, feet apart and dancing from foot to foot as a prize fighter might, although he did not hold up his fists. His speculative look asked me what I would do now.

It was obvious that, unless I removed Sam, the rest of the day would be the same chaotic struggle. The other children would have still another school day of learning nothing. After losing six weeks of school already this year, they could ill afford to lose more.

Accordingly, I called the main school while the children stood waiting. Sam looked smugly satisfied. Victory over another teacher was implicit in his expression as I asked for two messengers to come and escort Sam to the office. Although I wouldn't be able to resort to calling the office often, at least I could try to establish some rapport with the rest of the class today. Hopefully, we could begin creating an atmosphere in which the children could learn.

After the messengers left, with Sam regally escorted between them, I spent the little amount of time left before lunch trying to talk with the other children. The very most important rule in our class, I told them, was that no one was to hurt anyone else. I explained that I meant hurting others physically, hurting their feelings, or taking away others' learning time. Learning is fun, I added, and I wanted them to have fun. They sat passively, showing no interest in what I was saying, or perhaps in disbelief.

I gave up my sermon and encouraged them to talk about themselves, but Debra exuded hostility, and most of the others were taciturn or shy, evidently feeling they had nothing of value to say. Unfortunately, their experiences in life had taught them they were not of value. They had been separated from their peers, shunted from one teacher to another, or separated and put into different classrooms when no teacher was available for them. There was no teaching plan for them in any classroom.

This was 1969, in a city whose school system was considered to be advanced. Mentally handicapped children had just reached national attention in that decade. Earlier, a little progress had been made in developing strategies and techniques for teaching the retarded. Parents had organized the National Association for Retarded Children in 1950. That organization, now called Association for Retarded Citizens of the United States (ARC), had tried to answer the needs of retarded children and adults and to establish demonstration models for public and voluntary service agencies, but widespread national interest in the problems of the mentally handicapped had had to await the presidency of John F. Kennedy. In 1963, he had signed Public Law 98-164, providing for the organization of the Division of Handicapped Children and Youth within the United States Office of Education.

In 1964, the Elementary and Secondary Act had established grants from the federal government to state agencies for the purpose of providing free public education for handicapped children. Title I of this law provided services for disadvantaged handicapped children. Title II gave financial support to supplemental centers and encouraged the development of innovative programs for handicapped children.

In 1965 and 1966, two laws and an amendment provided more funds for schools aiding disadvantaged children and for establishing or expanding special programs for handicapped children. The Bureau of Education for Handicapped (BEH) was established within the United States Office of Education. This bureau allocated money to colleges, universities, and state departments of education, beginning in 1967. The money was to be used for preservice and in-service training of researchers and administrators of special education. Still, in 1969, the shortage of teachers, trained and willing to work in special education, was critical.

The new laws and organizations had helped, but the implementation and general knowledge of teaching techniques had lagged behind national interest. Also, there was a shortage of trained teachers and school psychologists in most areas, so a neglected class such as this one, unfortunately, was not unusual. No wonder many of these children had developed feelings of inadequacy and inferiority.

Harvey was an exception. He seemed to have retained some self-confidence, and he certainly didn't mind talking. In other circumstances, he would have been the class president. He had an appealing face which, except for Nellie's, wore the only real smile in the room. He was cautious around anyone with Sam's volatile nature, but kind and friendly with his other classmates. He had stretched an arm up and had placed it comfortably on Johnny's shoulder after the incident in the washroom, and I had noticed him trying to help Nellie draw her family earlier in the morning.

Harvey talked about all the different teachers they had had that year. I assured them that changing teachers was over. There would be no other teachers in this room this year. I was there to stay. Whether or not they believed me, or cared, was a moot question.

The lunch period hardly seemed long enough to get ready for the afternoon. I spent most of the time going through the cabinets at the rear of the room. Most of them were filled with old construction paper that crumbled at the edges when picked up, but one cabinet held some simple math papers, partially used workbooks, and a bonus of primers and several levels of readers from other reading series.

The early part of the afternoon was spent trying to find out what each child could do in math. Harvey and Nora had great difficulty copying problems from the chalkboard. The numbers ended up in odd places on the paper so that they no longer resembled problems, only numbers written at random on the paper, and making no sense as problems. Sheila shrieked in frustration periodically, while Debra steadily muttered her aversion to math and school in general. Kevin whined and Nellie hummed. With the exception of Norman, none of the children seemed to have any conception of what they were doing with these symbols.

Nellie and Verna were given the very simple papers I had found in the cabinet, but Verna was unable to handle them with or without help. One plus one was a foreign language. Fred was in his refuge under his desk. The children who finally finished their short math papers were told that they could read or put their heads down and rest. Several of them rested, and Verna fell fast asleep.

Norman's work, and a discussion with him, convinced me that he was far ahead of the others in math. He, like William, had just transferred to this school two weeks earlier, but Norman's records had not yet arrived. He appeared to be a studious boy, interested in learning, and not apt to play in class.

Harvey and Sheila became more and more restless as they struggled with their math problems until, at last, the recess bell rang to free us all. Verna slept on through recess.

The class returned from the playground bursting with excitement. Surprisingly, Debra, feeling secure in discovering a teacher's disapproval for someone other than herself, was the first to tell me that Sheila had been fighting. Sheila had hit a girl from the classroom next to ours, and she had been knocked down in retaliation.

"I'm gonna get my things, an' go home, an' get my Momma's gun, an' blow dat nigger's head off," Sheila bellowed. "She call me a scarface retard. My momma's not gonna like dat." She dug into her desk for the scarf she had worn to school that day. Papers, pencils, and crayons dropped to the floor.

I urged her into her chair and sat next to her with my hand on her shoulder, trying to soothe her.

"Sheila, it was not kind of the girl to say that, but you don't really mean what you're saying either." I patted her shoulder. "It hurts you when people say mean things to you. That's why we're not going to say those things in this room. Even if someone else is mean to us, we don't want to act the way they do. I know you don't want to be hurt, and you really don't want to hurt someone else."

Abruptly, she put her head down on her arm and began to sob. The fighting instinct had suddenly left her, and only her hurt feelings remained.

After I patted her shoulder a little while longer, her sobs gradually subsided, but she kept her head down on the curve of her arm. I took out a few of the books I had brought from home and read to the class. They were restless, but they listened, and the tension slowly began to decrease.

Sheila, emotionally drained, fell asleep. Verna slept through everything. The others drew for the last half-hour except for Fred, of course. He was safe in his turtle-like shell again.

The class was no longer chaotic, as it had been the rest of the day. It was as if Sheila's emotional draining had drained them all. I attributed this brief calm at the end of our day to their being as tired as I was.

18   *Retard*

Do the students know that teachers are sometimes as happy as they are when the school day is over?

II

A REAL BEGINNING

A tiny glint of interest showed in Debra's eyes the next day when she entered the classroom and saw the pile of "easy to read" books on my desk. But when I greeted her, she would neither look at me nor answer my greeting.

Harvey skipped in after her and answered my "good morning" cheerfully. He had visited me from outside the window before school, but that was our secret. If more of the children checked for my attendance each morning, I would never have time to prepare for the school day.

Johnny followed with a sheepish smile on his face. He had a smudge on his cheek already, and both of his shoelaces were trailing on the floor. He bumped into Debra's desk before he could reach his own.

"You a retard," Debra muttered to him audibly. I reminded her not to say anything if she couldn't say something nice, for which I drew the usual dark look.

The rest of the class followed somberly, except for Nellie, who wore her sweet open smile. Annabelle and Verna came in last, hand in hand. Each of them was painfully thin. Their hair was braided tightly to their heads in "corn rows," making them look like two large pairs of eyes mounted onto two pipe cleaner bodies. Verna was a smaller mirror image of eight-year-old Annabelle.

Sam was absent.

We began the day with reading. A review of the vocabulary and parts of a few stories in the primer verified that Debra, Norman, William, and Sheila knew the vocabulary. Except for Sheila, they demonstrated complete understanding of what they had read. Sheila was so indifferent and so easily distracted that it was difficult to tell if she couldn't concentrate, if she was not interested, or if she lacked comprehension.

The stories they were reading were so simple and humdrum that comprehension seemed automatic unless the children were just word calling, which wouldn't be surprising. The material they read was certainly not relevant to their lives. It was amazing that they could even summon the interest to read about Spot's being given a bath when it was frequently difficult for them to be given a bath.

Many families in the area had to share a bathroom with other families. Then their plumbing may or may not have worked. Given the realities of their lives, it was ridiculous to expect them to be too interested in whether or not a dog got a bath.

In spite of their problems, three of the four were anxious to show me that this book was easy for them to read. Even

Sheila got into the spirit of trying harder when she heard that her reading would earn a new book for her right then. Indifferent or not, a new reading book brought Sheila prestige.

They were each given a first grade reader in the same series. They all appeared to be pleased, although Debra tried to look indifferent. Sheila shrieked, of course, when she received hers. A reader in the same series was, unfortunately, all I had to give them.

Norman was more capable and more mature than the others. He was a very quiet nine-year-old boy who kept the others at a distance and showed no desire to talk or play with his classmates. He ignored the friendly advances of Harvey and Johnny. I knew he had transferred from another school in the same city, but he acted as if he had come from another country where a different language was spoken. He did his work quietly and neatly; work that didn't satisfy him he tore up and redid.

He had demonstrated a much more advanced knowledge of math the day before, but my questions about his previous class had been evaded. There was no doubt that he did not want to talk about his former school. Another teacher, who knew a teacher in that school, said he reputedly had a violent temper and had gotten into trouble because of it, but he had shown no signs of it here.

Since his records had not come, there was no additional information about him to help me speed up the process of finding the correct working level for his abilities. Advancing him to an area that was beyond his capability would discourage him, so we moved forward slowly but without repetition. So far, repetition had not been necessary for him, which indicated he had covered these types of math problems before.

Sheila was also nine but only showed an interest in reading or math when she was the center of attention. She changed from boredom with reading one minute to wild exuberance the next. She often punctuated her seat work with loud spontaneous comments or shrieks. Some of the other children would then jump in surprise, although they must have heard her shriek many times before this.

Her work varied from neat and legible to scrawly and messy. Generally, it was in the latter category. Though all the work given the children was necessarily broken into short segments, her attention span was even shorter than these tasks. She often had to be reminded to complete her work.

The four children who received new books were told to work on a short writing paper by copying a "morning story" which I had put on the chalkboard. When they finished it, they were told they could each pick out one of the books that I had brought from home and read quietly to themselves. The books had been carefully selected as the type that might help them read for enjoyment since they had few, if any, books at home.

From now on, they would be allowed to read at will in class whenever their assigned work was done. It was late in their young lives to start fostering a love of reading, but with encouragement, perhaps the love of reading could be nurtured in some of them. Debra had evinced a little interest already. Norman seemed to walk back to his seat more purposefully when he was told he could pick out a book to read after his work was finished.

Debra still muttered interminably throughout this second day, and Sheila still made loud comments, but both distractions seemed less vehement than they had the day before. Either they were getting acclimated, I was getting accustomed to them, or each of us was adjusting a little to the other.

Nora, Annabelle, Johnny, Kevin, and Harvey read slowly and somewhat unsteadily in their primer. It was obvious that they had read it before but had forgotten some of the words.

The words seemed to move around for Harvey, in that, while reading on one line, he would abruptly drop down to the middle of the line below. He reversed words, such as was and saw, and skipped both words and whole lines, looking bewildered when his reading made no sense. Nora had the same problems to a lesser degree. After this day, they would have to work separately from the rest of the class. It was obvious they had perceptual problems that the other children did not have and that they would need a special kind of help.

The other three students, Annabelle, Johnny, and Kevin, looked up after almost every word for assurance that they were reading correctly. Apparently, their reading experiences had been demoralizing enough for them to be constantly afraid of failure. Somehow, they had become a self-judging group and they judged that they were failures. They had no way of knowing that many circumstances had worked to keep them from being successful. They felt they were responsible for their own failure.

Suddenly, Nora put her head down on the reading table. When she was asked what was wrong, she said, "I just feel sort of funny, like I can't hold my head up." She squeezed her eyes shut to stop the tears that seeped out and across her anemic-looking cheeks.

At my request, Harvey brought a carton of milk from the chalkboard ledge and gave it to Nora. A few questions made it evident that neither Nora nor several of the others had had anything to eat that morning. Harvey had eaten some candy, and Sheila had eaten potato chips for their breakfast.

Milk cartons were always brought to the classrooms at the beginning of each school day for those who had brought their twenty cents milk money to school the previous Friday. Milk was usually given out around ten o'clock, making a slight diversion in the morning. After that day we had our milk first, and all the children received milk since, somehow, there were always extras. If the children ever wondered where the extra milk came from, they never asked.

In previous teaching years, I had seen hungry, poorly clad, sometimes abused or neglected children, but they never made up as large a proportion of the class as in this room. During the first year of my teaching, I had had so many nightmares about some of the children in my class that I had had to develop a philosophy that I might help some of them on their way out of this environment each year. I hoped other teachers would reach the ones I hadn't been able to help significantly.

Learning was impossible when a child was hungry or cold. Fortunately, friends of mine with children of their own had helped keep my other classes warmly dressed with clothes that their own children had outgrown. They would help again this year.

Learning was the only way these children could help themselves achieve a better future. Giving them the courage and the desire to keep trying to learn would make a difference in their lives, but even some of the youngest children seemed set in a pattern of despair, making it more difficult to help them.

Annabelle's sole interest in the classroom seemed to be taking care of her sister, Verna. I couldn't help but be grateful for this in the days that followed, since Verna was far from completely toilet trained. However, I did move Annabelle up next to Debra and away from Verna, hoping that Annabelle's concentration would no longer be focused on Verna's care. Verna was given permission to tell her sister any time she had to go to the bathroom. She didn't have the courage to tell me herself.

Annabelle, in her new spot, could not see her sister without turning around and so would hopefully give more of her attention to learning. At the age of eight, her role of being docile and motherly seemed well established. During any activities that were not related to Verna, her actions seemed tinged with a fear of being reprimanded. It was obvious that this child was confident about her "mothering" capabilities. Now she had to develop confidence in her learning capabilities.

The move was planned to be doubly productive, however. It also moved Sheila further from Debra so that, hopefully, the mutterings of the one would not bring out the shrieks of the other, and we would have fewer distractions. It also freed Annabelle from focusing on her child care duties.

Kevin did not seem fearful, as Annabelle did, but he was indifferent about school and inclined to whine. "It's too hard," and "I can't do it," were the first words he spoke regarding any type of work. He was almost eight but very immature and easily distracted. Affection seemed to be the only way to motivate him. A pat on the shoulder and a little praise would send him back to work for a brief period, only to be mesmerized again by some unseen vision.

He and his grandmother lived alone together with sporadic visits from his mother. His grandmother cared for him well physically. He was always well fed and neatly dressed, but he was starved for attention and for friends.

When these five children had taken their work back to their seats, I walked back to nine-year-old Fred's desk to see if he had accomplished anything. When he had entered the room that morning, I had waylaid him before he could get under his desk, thus ensuring that he sat on his chair as the other children did. I had given him a paper with the primary color words written inside giant balls for him to color appropriately.

As I drew near him, it became easy to guess why his desk was in the rear of the room. The smell of urine was so strong that it took an act of will to ignore it and stand near enough to check his work. He and his father lived alone. I decided I would have to call the father and ask him to come in for a talk about Fred. No child should have to be so unnecessarily unappealing to his fellow classmates.

I had brought in a box of tissues so that he could wipe his constantly running nose, but I found that I had to tell him to make use of them each time they were needed. He seemed to have no sensation from the runny nose, or perhaps the feeling had become natural to him.

To my surprise, he had attempted to follow my directions with his crayons. Two of the primary colors were scrawled over the appropriate balls. He either could read the color words or had remembered what I had said earlier, either of which was encouraging. And he was still seated in his chair.

The Intelligence Quotient range in the classroom was recorded as a span of from 55 to 75. Fred, Nellie, and Verna were in the lower range. Even the most handicapped children in this class could at least be taught to maintain cleanliness, do simple tasks, and learn the words they needed to know for their safety and survival. Given the proper training, their language skills and coordination should be improved enough so that they could eventually work in a sheltered workshop type of environment.

I praised Fred for his work, and his eyes glanced at me furtively from under his lowered eyebrows. He appeared tense. His face was tinged with old, sooty dirt. I handed him soap and two paper towels, noticing as he took them that his fingernails were bitten well beyond the quick. He was then sent to the washroom to wash his face and hands. His grayish complexion had lightened considerably, overall, and his high bony forehead almost shone when he returned.

Fred was painfully thin and walked in a disjointed manner that made you wonder if his muscles would collapse before the next step was completed. His clothes seemed to flap about him, adding to the fragile, storklike figure he presented.

Nellie was the exact opposite of Fred. She was always scrubbed clean in the morning. Her hair was combed and frequently tied with a bright ribbon. Her clothes were washed and ironed. Her happy disposition bespoke loving care. She would work at the same task over and over again without becoming bored or restless. She had no apparent fear of failure, making her the exception in this class of fearful children.

Nellie's mother was justifiably protective and walked her to and from school each day. She had introduced herself to me as the children left school the previous day.

Verna, like Nellie, tried to do what she was asked, but her attention span was so short that she was frequently diverted by the activities or the comments of the others. Most of her time was spent timidly trying to watch the other children without it being noticed that she was doing so. The question, "What you starin' at, Retard?" from Debra had been enough to keep Verna's head down for an hour.

Any questions directed at Verna brought an expression of frantic fear to her face. If she answered at all, it was in a whispered monosyllable. She was obviously less comfortable without her sister next to her and looked up every few minutes to make sure that Annabelle was still in the room. She would never be a discipline problem, but finding appropriate activities to stimulate her mental growth and muscular coordination would be a challenge.

Because most of the children had such short attention spans, we used short action poems or exercise games several times throughout the day. The poems allowed the children to stretch and move around, which relaxed them.

"Simon Says" was the most beneficial action game for them because so many concepts could be incorporated into it. The most important concept for them right now was to learn the difference between left and right. This was particularly difficult for many of the children to learn, and the varied repetition in the activities of that old standby helped, while simultaneously relieving the tension between learning tasks.

Over all, our second day was productive. It certainly couldn't have been called a peaceful class, but the room did not hold the high tension it had the day before when Sam was present. Most of the children "tried me out" to see how far they could go, and they verbally picked at each other occasionally; but the vibrant spirit of animosity was noticeably weaker and they didn't need to be constantly alert to the physical menace of Sam.

We got to know each other a little that second day, and part of our class routine was developed. The security of a routine would help these children settle down and relax. They needed simple rules to follow constantly since there had been little consistency in their lives. It would be soothing for them to know what to expect in class each day, as long as our routine wasn't too rigid and they weren't expected to fit into an exact mold.

Friday morning Sam reappeared, jostling the others as he came in and giving me a defiant look. I was as prepared for him as possible. When we had changed Annabelle's and Sheila's desks, the day before, I moved Sam's desk to the right of mine and well in front of the other children's desks. The classroom was designed for a larger number of children, and we could easily have large empty areas. There was room for a large neutral zone around Sam, and I took advantage of it. The reading table was behind and to the left of me so that, by moving my chair back, I could sit with each reading group and still keep an eye on Sam.

Sam again refused to read to me, pushing the book off his desk and kicking it away when I encouraged him to read. I could not tell if he was unable to read or if he was so sure of criticism that he wouldn't try. In desperation, I gave him some of the color word papers that Nellie and Fred were doing and tried to concentrate on the reading group.

Norman had printed the new vocabulary words legibly on the chalkboard for himself and the rest of his group, which included William, Debra, and Sheila. The group proceeded to read their story well. Debra's facial muscles were slightly more relaxed that day, and each of the four was pleased with his/her own performance.

After praising them, I told them to read on in their books when they had finished their written work, and to ask me if they were not sure of any of the words. They were yielding their seats at the reading table to the next reading group when Nellie cried out.

Having been given a few seconds without my attention partially on him, Sam had whipped over and pulled Nellie's hair ribbon off, catching a wisp of her hair in the process and painfully pulling it, too. When I crossed behind my desk on my way toward Sam, the children apparently thought I was going to the teacher's closet. A long "oooo-ooooh" sounded from the class. Sam plopped down in his chair, as if shoved by an unseen hand. He eyed me uneasily.

"Why the big 'oh'?" I asked.

"Dat's where da' last teacher kep' da' stick to use on Sam," Sheila volunteered. The others chorused agreement. Whether or not that stick had ever been used, I noticed Sam certainly reacted more to the thought of it than he had to my admonitions. However, used or unused, the presence of a stick had certainly not improved his deportment permanently. Was this type of punishment what had made him so calloused about causing pain for others?

"There is no stick in the closet now; no one should use a stick on anyone else," I said. "This is our class, and we should be kind to one another. We will be spending every day together and we should make each other feel good so we'll all be happy. No one is happy who makes someone else unhappy."

I would find myself repeating the themes of being kind to each other and having pride in their work almost daily. The children were so accustomed to criticism that they either attacked someone else to distract attention from their own problems or they were reluctant to try new learning experiences for fear they would fail while attempting to master them.

Sam's face was a blank-eyed mask. No words seemed able to enter and penetrate his defenses. He did not return after lunch. Because of their financial need, lunch was provided for all of the children in this group by the government. The other children said he often left after eating his lunch. But I wondered if he thought the stick was really still in the closet, waiting for his next misdeed.

All of Sam's energy was directed toward controlling the other children by making them fear him. That fear gave him a feeling of power. My accidental move toward the teacher's closet, which apparently implied the possible use of a stick, had taken that power away from him thereby making him lose face, and possibly encouraging him to leave for the day.

Perhaps because of the tension of Sam's morning attendance or perhaps just because it was Friday, the children were even more restless that afternoon. Each of the children displayed his or her own reaction to tension. Debra's reaction was to attack someone else. I had to move Annabelle's desk again when Debra's muttered insults reduced her to tears. Debra muttered at her closest neighbor as relentlessly as a steam shovel, digging up real or imagined flaws the victim hoped were buried.

Johnny was so amiable and peaceful that I put him next to Debra, hoping she would see no reason to attack him. There was nothing threatening about Johnny to inspire her malice. The prospect of physical aggression affected him visibly, but verbal abuse had not seemed to bother him. He had ignored being called a 'retard' by Debra the previous day. Fred was back under his desk, where he had holed up in the morning when Sam arrived. Verna had tears running down her face for no apparent reason other than the pain of her sister's hurt feelings. Harvey played jack-in-the-box—up to sharpen a pencil, up to look out the window, up to get another piece of paper. Only Nellie stayed the same and softly hummed to herself, her pulled hair completely forgotten.

It would have been nice to have a tape recording of my voice saying, "Harvey, sit down. Fred, wipe your nose. Johnny, tie your shoes. Debra, be kind. Sheila, don't shriek. Kevin, don't whine." The tape recording could then admonish the class and leave me free to do a few other things!

Fortunately, it was gym day for our class. That gave me some preparation time during the school day. While the children were with their gym teacher, I went over to the main school to get more advanced math material to use with Norman.

The office directed me to another teacher's classroom. This teacher taught the level of math in which Norman would be working and the supplies were kept in her room. I needed a teacher's guide for myself and workbook for him. The teacher looked somewhat irritated at the interruption.

"What makes you think you can use a third grade workbook with someone in that class?" she asked sarcastically, but she went to the back of the room to get the books from a cabinet without waiting for a reply.

While I waited for her to get them, some brave child whom I had taught in a previous year, whispered hello to me. This brought an immediate tirade from the teacher. Her face was taut with anger.

"Quiet!" She turned to me. "Look at them! Just look at them!" Her voice rasped with derision. "How can you teach them anything? They're all *stupid*. They don't even know how to behave in school. They'll never learn anything!"

"Oh, no, I'm sure you have many good students," I murmured inadequately. She looked at me sharply. Then her eyes dismissed me. Unaccountably, I felt guilty, sharing the feeling of the class, silenced by fear. I was as embarrassed and shaken as the students at her outburst, maybe more so since I had not heard such tirades over and over again. I hurried to thank her for the math books and left. I wondered if the children in my class had experienced this same type of treatment from this type of teacher. Was this where the children's confidence was stolen away, and replaced with apathy, fear, or hostility?

The teacher had spoken as if the children couldn't hear her or wouldn't be hurt by what she said. She was calloused to the misery she caused. I was appalled that I had been unable to think of more to say to help the children save their pride and self-confidence.

That teacher, and several other teachers in the school, had taught different types of children throughout the years at this school. The neighborhood had changed several times, one group of people succeeding another. The greatest part of their teaching time had been spent teaching immigrants' children who had been imbued with the importance of getting an education in this strange land. Going to school was a serious matter to them.

It seemed difficult for some of these teachers to adjust to a different type of child, a child who perhaps had no prepa-

A Real Beginning 35

ration for education and who might be more interested in socializing in class. To these teachers, all noise was bad. It disrupted the regimen they had developed over the years. It grated on their nerves. The combination of their rigid classroom standards with children who sometimes did not realize the importance of education brought out common feelings in the teacher and the students. Unfortunately, they were negative feelings about the children's educational ability.

All too easily children absorb the opinions of others and decide they can't be taught. I thought of Nora, Annabelle, and Johnny. Had they heard the type of comments I just heard and become overly timid? Or had Sam, Debra, and Sheila heard comments that made them hostile?

***

When I got back to the annex, the children had left the gym and were having recess on the playground. I stopped and watched the way they interacted with their peers.

Debra was jumping a rope that was swung by Sheila and another tall girl, the girl that Sheila had been ready to shoot just two days earlier. Fierce little Debra was telling them both how she wanted the rope swung.

Harvey played ball with some other boys, but Johnny flinched whenever the ball was thrown to him. Because of his slower coordination, the ball hit him. He moved away from the area, tripping over his shoelaces as he went.

Fred crouched against the wall of the school, looking at the ground. No one bothered him, and he bothered no one.

Norman walked quietly around the edge of the playground, thinking weighty thoughts. He was oblivious to the laughter and activity around him.

Annabelle and Verna stood, hand in hand, as if looking in a candy store window, watching the other children play. Verna was the youngest of all the children in the annex. She had no one who was her age to play with, but surely Annabelle would have liked to have played with some others. Nellie stood near them, smiling serenely and watching the other children with no apparent desire to join in the games.

Kevin and William were talking quietly to a boy from another class. Kevin took a coin from his pocket and gave it to the boy. I had seem him give William a nickel the day before and wondered if he were trying to buy new friends.

Nora played jump rope with two girls from another class. She did not play with the same spirit some of the others showed, however. Her play had the same docile, solemn quality that marked her classroom behavior.

After recess, I read to the class. Even Harvey, who jumped up to look out the window when a car honked, then had to get up again to throw away a scrap of paper, finally sat still and listened. He and I had decided the day before that he would only do his handstands and flips at the end of the school day. As proud as he was of them, today he forgot them entirely. We had made a slight adjustment in his hyperactivity.

When the bell rang, I walked the children to the door. Nellie's mother was waiting, as usual.

Out by the curb, another woman waited. She was dressed all in black. Her black hose and five-inch heels, plus the long, fake-fur boa hanging around her shoulders, made a strange contrast to the young children happily tumbling out the school door.

As I watched, Nora went up to her. She handed Nora something shiny that looked like a key and said a few words to her, giving Nora's shoulder a little shove at the same time to send her on her way.

I asked Nellie's mother who the woman was.

"She's Nora's mother." At my surprised look, she added gregariously, "Oh, yes I've known her almost all her life. I know almost everyone around here. She's a hard one. She's had to be. When she turned fourteen, her mother gave her to Nora's father. Sold her to him probably. He left Nora's mother less than a year later, when she was big with Nora. She had Nora before her fifteenth birthday. She's been on her own ever since then."

"That means she's not quite twenty-two now." I'm sure my skepticism showed. She looked at least thirty-five in spite of a liberal application of make-up.

"That's right," Nellie's mother said. "She's not much more than a child herself."

Children were raising children here, I thought.

As we talked, Nora's mother turned and got into an old car where a man waited for her. They pulled away without a glance at Nora.

Nora was walking slowly away from the school. Her head was down and her feet dragged. She looked abandoned. It appeared that she was going home to an empty apartment. She had no brothers or sisters. Nellie's mother said that her grandparents and the rest of the family had moved away before Nora was born.

―――

Sam never came back to the annex. The following Monday, I was notified by the office that he had been transferred to the boys' correctional school for disciplinary problems. I felt badly that I had been unable to do anything for him and hoped there would be someone in his new school who could reach him. The student/teacher ratio would have to be quite low to teach that type of child, and at the same time protect each child from the other children. I didn't know if Sam was mentally handicapped, had only emotional problems, had social problems, or if all three factors were involved. If he had more than one problem, which one developed first and what were the causes? Which problem should you address first?

It seemed the EMH classroom was being used for children with social and/or emotional problems, children with learning disabilities, and children who were mentally handicapped. We now know that learning disabilities are problems in one or more of the basic psychological processes involved in understanding or using language, causing difficulties in some areas of the ability to listen, think, speak, read, write, spell, or do math. Learning disabilities do not include mental retardation. A learning disabled child can have an average or above average IQ. They do not need the same type of instruction that mentally handicapped children need.

The diversity of problems gathered in one classroom made it more difficult to help each child learn as much as possible. They all needed individual help, so a time juggling situation developed. Nothing in teacher training courses prepared you for a class like this.

III

UNNECESSARY HANDICAPS

Phonic charts with pictures and words to illustrate the sounds, pictures of the seasons, a chart with the days of the week, and other visual aids were hung, joining the ever present alphabet cards that crowned every chalkboard. The added colors made the room look more cheerful, and I climbed down from my chair with a feeling of satisfaction. I was about to relax for a minute before school began when William's mother strode into the classroom.

She was an attractive, nicely dressed woman whom I had spoken to several times two years earlier when William was in my first grade class. She had been recalcitrant then and unable or unwilling to listen to my pleas that William attend school more regularly. Nothing I had said had convinced her of the importance of his being in class consistently.

"First, William has a different teacher every day. Then, he has his first grade teacher again. Has he been put all the way back to first grade?" Her voice was vibrating with hostility.

"No, Mrs. Andrews, this is a special class, just as William was in a special class part of last year in Jones school."

There was no need to verbally remind her that he had been judged mentally handicapped.

"He says he's already had both of the reading books you're using here, so I took time off work to come in and tell you."

"I'm sure he could have had these books before. We will review the second one as quickly as possible, to be sure that he knows all the words. He is doing well with it and will have another book as soon as he has mastered the vocabulary in this one." I wanted to be encouraging, but I couldn't resist adding, "I hope William's health has improved enough so he can come to school regularly now. That will help him learn more quickly."

"He'll be here every day," she said, and marched out.

If William were really sick, of course he should be taken care of at home, but I was sure he had stayed at home without cause when he was in first grade. The shock of finding him at the seemingly same spot that he had been in two years before might ensure his coming to school regularly now. I wondered if that handsome little boy would be in this class now if he had attended school regularly the previous years?

He was a little slower than average, perhaps, but he could have learned in a regular classroom, if he had expended more effort to learn and if he had been in school more often. When I had taught him in first grade, he had seemed to be babied, and he certainly had not wanted to do any schoolwork. Since he had transferred shortly after the first semester, I didn't know whether or not he had attended school regularly at his other school. I had not yet gone through his file.

Children who are habitually lazy because too little has been expected of them frequently perform less successfully than they could on intelligence tests. Anxiety can also cost a test taker seven or eight IQ points, and language differences certainly cause some variation in scores. All these factors, plus the fact that only one test was given to each student, made correct placement in the EMH classrooms questionable at times.

In the regular classroom, children hobbled by poverty were frequently two years behind the average child after a few years in school. If William had expended some real effort, he would be no further behind than some of the students in the regular classrooms. As I was thinking about this, the opening bell rang.

The children marched in, and the new week began. A few said, "Good morning, Teacher," in response to my greeting, and a few looked up and smiled that day. That week and the week that followed comprised our shake-down cruise.

By the end of these two weeks, we had established a fairly consistent routine. The children had become comfortable with it, and more comfortable with me. It was still not the type of classroom it could be, but we were headed toward a better atmosphere.

Harvey still checked at the open classroom window often, his warm bright eyes appearing over the windowsill after his call of "Teacher." After he was sure I was there, he shared some news with me before school. He calmed down some in class, as did the others. His early morning visits made him feel important and established a bond between us.

The same teacher every day and a familiar routine helped all of the children. Too much routine can be boring but mentally handicapped or disturbed children need more routine than others. Change was more difficult for them, and they needed to know that each day would be similar to the day before. They also needed to be prepared for any necessary changes that would be coming their way.

Nora became lightheaded again in class, as did Annabelle, so we started having breakfast as well as their milk on some days. I brought individual boxes of cereal occasionally, and hard boiled eggs for the class some other mornings. The eggs were supplemented with doughnuts, which we shopped for together.

There was a bakery outlet two blocks away, and we had received permission to walk to this bakery occasionally in the afternoon. Besides being a way to get our breakfast doughnuts, the walks were used as a reward for good behavior.

The walks also helped the children learn to walk together in a safe and orderly manner and to notice and read signs in their neighborhood. It took longer than believable, at first, to get them to walk together in any way that resembled order. I was dismayed at our willy-nilly appearance. The disparity in heights, since there was an almost five-year age span, made our column resemble a centipede moving along, humping up in some spots and close to the ground in others. Added to that, uneven walking tempos, plus fretful quarreling made our first walk comic at best. A sense of humor is sometimes a teacher's only salvation.

Gradually, the more aggressive children relaxed, and the timid grew brave until we could walk to the bakery or over to the main school for an assembly in a somewhat orderly manner. We even made it out onto the playground for a fire drill without too many problems. Our next lesson, however, had to be on how to calm down after a variation in our normal routine.

One morning before school, while breakfast was still an occasional treat, Harvey hiked himself up to our window.

"Teacher, we has breakfas' dis mornin?" His eager expression told me he felt both hunger and hopefulness. I was angry with myself for letting him down.

"No, Harvey, I had nothing to bring this morning except hard-boiled eggs. I was afraid they would be too dry all alone so I didn't bring them."

His eyes widened and took on a soft wistful quality.

"Oh, Teacher, jus' an egg," he said, with obvious longing.

"Harvey, don't you ever have eggs at home?"

"Sometime we has a few. But eggs is for cakes." He was so earnest with his explanation that I knew he had been given that explanation many times and had given the matter a good deal of thought.

We had breakfast daily after that morning conversation. I was a little apprehensive at first, afraid that they would think each morning was a party, and would waste some of their precious learning time. But it was surprising how quickly they settled down to work after a little breakfast. A few of the children ate breakfast at home, but they never turned down a second one.

No child ever spoke up and said they were hungry. Hunger was treated as an accepted condition of life. It was something you just lived with.

This was the year before the school breakfast program for disadvantaged children began. That most fortunate law helped many children achieve more in school.

Our breakfast became a family meal. We would talk about something that was happening in their lives while they ate. From our conversation or something else that interested them, we would use the time to compose our short morning story. As many new vocabulary words as possible would be included in it. When the story was written on the board, it became their writing assignment.

Gradually, more children than Harvey and Sheila contributed to the stories, and some of them began to show a little improvement in expressing themselves. When a particular interest of theirs was the focal point of our conversation, their ability to communicate increased even more, and they developed more confidence in themselves.

After breakfast became a regular part of our day, Harvey was more contented. He lost some of his jack-in-the-box quality that had distracted the others. He was able to sit quietly and read or write for longer periods of time.

Annabelle lost some of her apathy, either because of the extra food or from familiarity with the class. Even little Verna looked a tiny bit more lively.

Annabelle actually whispered to Nellie one day and, on another occasion, to Nora. She had thought of something to say and had dared to say it. It was so delightful to see her emerge from her self-woven cocoon that I didn't even consider asking her to be quiet. Silence is not always golden!

In many large public school systems in the past, classes were judged by how quiet they were. While there must be a quiet atmosphere for the students to be able to concentrate, too much emphasis on quiet and control diminished the children's enthusiasm for learning, however. Many of the students learned to sit still and be silent only in order to survive and avoid the catastrophe of ridicule. Some of them became apathetic or, as in Sam's case perhaps, developed a strong hostility toward school. It was too emotionally painful for some of them to try to succeed by speaking up in class and still be called bad or stupid, so they lost interest and tried to be unobtrusive to avoid criticism.

By the time they entered school, the children in this neighborhood were almost always behind their peers in more affluent neighborhoods. They were not exposed to many of the things common to other children, such as large stores, parks, libraries, varied architectural designs and different transportation systems. Also, they lacked the books and magazines at home that would have expanded their horizons, so they lost more time learning what their peers already knew. The process of adjusting to school cost them even more time. Children who are truly mentally handicapped frequently have more difficulty adjusting to new situations than the so-called average child. I did not want my timid children to become even more withdrawn, or the more spontaneous ones, such as Harvey, to become hostile to school. It was important for them to enjoy school and learning, as long as their enjoyment did not distract others who were trying to learn. They also needed the experience of working with each other constructively.

There was no one I could find to work with Fred, however. No one wanted to be near him. His father would have to improve Fred's hygiene. Fortunately, a second note to his father brought results. He appeared hesitantly in our doorway one day.

Fred's father worked nights as a bartender. It therefore cost him an extra effort to come to school during what was normally his sleeping time. It was possible that he didn't see Fred before Fred left for school each day, or perhaps he had begun to think Fred's grooming and behavior were normal.

Life had not been easy for this pale shaky man. Several years earlier, his wife had left him with two boys to raise. Two years ago, Fred's older brother hanged himself. The brother had been twelve at the time and was considered by school personnel to be an average, normal boy. No one knew what terrible despair had caused him to become so desperate as to take his own life.

To compound the tragedy, Fred had come home after school and had discovered the body. He was already a member of the EMH class at the time, but no one remembered now whether or not his behavior before his brother's death had been as bizarre as it now was.

Perhaps it was too painful for Fred's father to let himself care for his second son after the loss of his other loved ones, but he would have to take more of an interest. He needed to help Fred learn to bathe himself, and to do so regularly. There was a good possibility that the bathroom they used was shared with other families, but if he tried sufficiently, some method could be worked out. Also, he had to help Fred remember to wipe his nose when he needed to, and to remember to comb his hair.

Six hours a day in school were not enough to accomplish all the training Fred needed. If he did not get more help than he was getting, Fred would become a custodial case when he got older or if something happened to his father. They did not seem to have too much time together, but since there was no one else in the home, working with Fred might bring the two closer together.

Fred's father stood in the hallway just outside the classroom door. He smiled uncertainly and nodded at everything said to him. But, somehow, he looked empty, and I wondered if he had the same ability to tune out the world that Fred had.

Fred spent most of his days sitting at his desk now instead of under it. He sat there by choice, but he still behaved more like a wary animal would than an almost ten-year-old boy. The smell of urine haloing him and his peculiar behavior isolated him from his fellow schoolmates.

The children from the other classrooms called him "Crazy Horse" because he would sometimes canter around the playground "neighing," and then return to crouch in his shell against the school wall. The other children never bothered him, perhaps because he acted so strangely.

Nellie's home life was entirely different from Fred's. It was evident from her manner that she had a happy home and was not left alone in it, as Fred and Nora were in theirs.

Nellie's mother came into the classroom to visit several afternoons when school was almost over. Her loving care and, from what she said, her husband's concern for Nellie had brought out the best in Nellie by freeing her from the restraints of fear and lack of confidence in herself.

Nellie's mother always brought the other children cookies. She was a sweet-faced, gray-haired woman with a comfortable figure. Warmth and cookies would be common in her home.

She had trained Nellie to bathe herself and dress herself and to do simple household chores, she told me. She hoped that, if anything should happen to her and her husband, Nellie would be able to take care of herself. It was easy to see that her life revolved around her home and her family.

Nellie and Fred mastered the words stop and go. They could identify the words when they were mixed in with other words and were quite proud of their accomplishment. Fred truly enjoyed his "reading" and would bellow out the words in a surprisingly deep voice. The loudness and deepness of it contrasted so sharply with his soft whispering to his fingers and his high-pitched giggle when talking to his fingers that it was startling. He did not giggle with the other children, nor did he even talk to them.

They had also mastered a few of the color words, and I gave each a second pre-primer so they could feel they were making some progress. They knew the first one by heart, reciting it from memory with barely a glance at the pages. It was not reading, at best it was word calling, but it made them feel better about themselves.

Verna came to the reading table with her pre-primer for a brief period when they did. She couldn't read, but she could identify the boy and girl in the stories. She participated so she would not be the only one in the room without a book and would know that someday she would read.

In Fred's case particularly, I wondered if too little might have been expected of him or if he had regressed after the shock of his brother's suicide. One day, when we were to be observed by some student teachers, he was whispering to his fingers and giggling softly. A beginning math paper was on his desk and I knew he was capable of doing the problems on it. I told him to stop acting silly and to get to work.

Some secret awareness flickered in his eyes. He gave me a little surprised smile, picked up his pencil, and went to work. He had been hiding behind his "Crazy Horse" act to escape the work and anxieties of his world. I wondered what he could have achieved in his earlier years without the external problems he had in addition to being mentally handicapped. Support and encouragement might have made a tremendous difference in his development.

Unnecessary Handicaps 51

Verna worked on color words with Fred and Nellie. She was so much younger, though, that it would take a lot of repetition for her really to learn them. The three of them sorted beads by color, and they were beginning to try to sort them by shape, as a learning process for mastering discrimination.

With blunt-ended scissors, the three of them were often busy cutting out pictures of dogs, cats, mothers, fathers, and other categories that were within their realm of experience and pasting them on construction paper. Many times, only part of an animal or person escaped the ravages of their scissors, and it took a good deal of imagination for me to discover the appropriate title to print on the top of the paper. Although their activities were at the most simple level, seeing the same words over and over again would eventually make them familiar to them. Verna still tired easily and frequently fell asleep during some of their activities.

One day, when I was cleaning Verna up after one of her accidents, I noticed tiny white scars running up the back of one leg. They were evenly spaced, like the teeth of a large zipper. When I asked her what had made the scars on her leg, she whispered, "Rat!"

Annabelle told me later that, when Verna was smaller, a rat had hidden in her bed. When Verna climbed into the bed, it bit her several times before her cries brought help. Annabelle, who had been so very shy when the school year began, had now become quite brave about talking to me.

When Annabelle was coming in from the playground one day, she turned her ankle and her shoe fell off. She was wearing "Mary Janes" with the straps cut off so they just slipped on, as loafers do. When she took a step to retrieve the shoe and put it on, her foot unfolded, and I could see that her toes had been completely doubled under in order for her foot to fit in the shoe. Walking with toes bent over to that extent must have been extremely painful. Just having the shoes on would be very uncomfortable. It was no longer surprising that she did not run and play or jump rope with the other children.

Friends of mine, who had slightly older children, sent an assortment of shoes to school the next day, and Annabelle then had shoes that were large enough for her. They sent her other clothing, as well, including a warm coat, and they sent clothing for the other children, too. Among the clothes was a suede jacket with fringe on the sleeves and pockets, like a cowboy jacket. Johnny was the only one who came close to its size, and he grew another two inches when he put it on. It was a struggle to get him to take it off in the warm classroom. It had to be hung on the back of his chair so everyone would know it was truly his.

Annabelle began to lose her pinched look. She was shyly proud of her new clothes, and she began to play with the others when she went out to recess. She would bounce a ball back and forth with Nellie and Verna. Her coordination was much better than theirs, and she actually laughed out loud once when she ran to catch one of Verna's wilder throws. They were a group now, no longer just standing and watching while other groups played.

The large ball had been brought for Nellie, Verna, and Fred to roll back and forth to each other in the back of the classroom. Many of the other things I had acquired to use in my first grade classes were in use here now. There were puzzles with large pieces, shoes to practice lacing and tying, beads to sort and string, and a balance board to "walk the plank" on. The latter was particularly important for Johnny to practice with since his coordination was very poor.

When the ball was taken out at recess time, I had to go out too, at least often enough so that the more aggressive children from other classes learned not to take the ball away from our class. My presence also helped the children in another way—the other classes were taught not to refer to "the dummy class" or the "retards" any more, plus going out to the playground provided me with an excellent opportunity to see what social progress the children were making.

The children who needed to socialize the most, except for Fred, were making gradual progress. Fred would roll the ball back and forth across the floor in the classroom with the others, now, but he could not be coaxed into taking part with them on the playground. He did watch them furtively, though. At least, his eyes were no longer glued to the ground.

IV

TWO STEPS FORWARD

During my previous years of teaching first graders, it had always thrilled me to see the delight with which children learned to read. Although some advanced more slowly than the others, there were none incapable of learning. To counteract the lack of reading stimulus in their homes, I had brought many books into the classroom. Summer library sales of old books and garage sales had been an inexpensive way to augment the primers and readers the school system provided. The use of these books helped in this class, too.

We had our own "lending library" that the children could borrow from when their class work was finished and from which they could choose a book to take home to read. These books came back, for the most part, to be exchanged for other books. Eventually, even some of the less able readers took simple books home. I tried to be sure they could read them well so that their families could see they were succeeding and would praise them. It seemed that each child stood a little straighter and looked a little more proud of himself when he had a book to take home.

We now had two goldfish to feed and to care for, a project Harvey in particular loved. He talked to the fish when he fed them and never minded taking someone else's turn to clean the fish bowl.

Each child had a turn caring for the fish. They also had turns at being "monitors" by handing out writing paper, paper towels, soap, and milk. They took turns cleaning the chalkboard and erasers. In fact, they had every job that I could think of, to develop responsibility and self-confidence.

I used a tape recorder to tape their reading when they were doing particularly well. Listening to the tapes of their own voices reading from their own reading books, delighted them more than anything else. The tape recorder even encouraged the less inclined readers, like Sheila and Kevin, to try harder. When they heard how well their reading sounded on tape, they were encouraged to take more of our library books home to read to their families. The sound of their own voices on tape was fascinating to them. It affirmed to them that they were really children of value. Hopefully, their families would reinforce this new feeling of worthiness that had been so long in coming to them.

Debra had become a little more comfortable in school, although she still muttered to or about anyone who irritated her. And she was easily irritated. She had a talent for finding each child's vulnerable spot. "Retard" was one of her favorite words, and I wondered how often it had been applied to her. I ignored her muttering the word " honky" when she was displeased with me, but continued to remind her not to hurt the other children's feelings. Her other *sotto voce* comments too often found their mark.

Fortunately, she was in the front seat on the side of the room, so she only had to have one person seated next to her, but there was almost no one left. Nellie was her current neighbor. Since Nellie was in her own special world most of the time, perhaps she could ignore Debra's comments. Johnny, with his peaceful nature, had finally shown he was being hurt by Debra's comments. Being called "burr-head" had been the final straw.

Debra wanted to test everyone. She was sure she would be rejected by all. She was so sure of animosity that she hurried to get in the first blow. When she was praised, she turned her triangular face at an angle and had a curious skeptical expression, as if wondering if she could really merit praise.

One day, after I praised her for helping Nellie pick up some crayons she had dropped, Debra said, "Momma say I'm bad." She gave me her questioning look, with her head tilted, much as a curious kitten would look.

"I don't think she really means you're bad, because you're not," I said. "Maybe she's tired when she says that. I know it makes you feel unhappy when she says it. That's how you make other people feel when you call them names. Now that you know how it makes people feel, I'm sure you won't want to do it anymore." She looked at me solemnly while she thought over that idea.

Someone in her home cared for her. Her clothes were always neat, and she was clean. Her hair was freshly braided, each day, standing out from her head as if starched. Helping Nellie pick up her crayons was the first time Debra had done something kind for someone else in the classroom. Perhaps she was beginning to see that others had needs and feelings, very much as she did.

Most of the other children were evincing better behavior now, too, and they seemed happier. Nora, however, was still more tired than she should have been. She was always anxious to please but she was listless, and occasionally fell asleep in class.

One day, she fell asleep just before recess, and I told the others to let her sleep while they went out to the playground. She awakened while they were still outside, and I took the opportunity of being alone with her to ask her how much sleep she got at night.

"Sometimes I don't get much sleep. There's a man who comes and bangs on our door at night. If I'm still up, my mother tells me to get in bed. She makes me cover up my head before she lets him in. He has a mean voice, and I'm afraid of him."

Whenever this man came, Nora said, she would lie in her bed, awake and frightened. Some nights she would be asleep before he came to their door, but his banging or his gruff voice would awaken her. She was sometimes afraid he was hurting her mother. His voice would keep her awake for a long time, and when she did fall asleep, she would have bad dreams. When she woke up, she still felt frightened. Even though the man would be gone, she could not stop worrying about him. She told me there were other men who came to their house to visit, but none of them were as loud or sounded as mean as this man who came so often.

Nothing could be done to help this child, except to pray that she kept hidden and was ignored by the men who came to her house. It was not unknown for daughters to be raped by their mother's boyfriends. If her mother knew that Nora had told a teacher about her problems, she might punish Nora, so nothing could be said to her mother.

It was difficult to accept that there were so many problems that could not be solved for the children. They were trying to find a safe place in their frightening, hostile world. Providing a peaceful, accepting atmosphere in the classroom, a sort of sanctuary for them, would soothe them and make them better able to learn. An education was the only permanent way to help them get out of their environment. A double effort had to be made to inspire each of them to succeed.

At the end of one school day, Nellie's mother came in to ask if she could have a birthday party for Nellie in the classroom on the following day. It was a great idea. In fact, with a class this small in number, it wouldn't be difficult to have a birthday party for each one of the children. The children who had summer birthdays could have their parties in late May or early June, before school was over for the year. A party of their own would make them feel more important since many of them had probably never had a birthday party. So we added birthday parties to our agenda.

Nellie's birthday party was a real success. Her mother created a feeling of sharing by bringing in balloons for all of the children. No one seemed to begrudge Nellie her special day.

Sheila was voted the champion at blowing up balloons. All of her shrieking must have built up her lung power. She blew up balloons for several of the less adept, as well as blowing up her own.

Before his balloon was tied, Harvey discovered that a balloon would fly across the room if released with some air in it. Soon everyone was imitating Harvey, and the noise level rose high enough that there was a possibility of disturbing other classes. Only the cake and ice cream waiting for them could induce the children to let me tie off the filled balloons while the air was still in them.

The children had made birthday cards for Nellie, and they sang "Happy Birthday" to her. She received a little bracelet as a gift from the whole class. Nellie sat and smiled the smile that would keep her forever young in appearance. Suddenly, however, her stomach rebelled, and all the cake and ice cream came up. It slithered over her desk and dripped to the floor beneath it. She looked around, confused at what had happened to her.

Before I could begin to react, Sheila was up getting out the paper towels. Nellie's mother took Nellie off to the washroom to clean her up. Surprisingly, Sheila insisted on helping me clean up the mess.

Even with the excitement causing Nellie to have an upset stomach, it had been a great way to end the week. We had a happy day, and a child who had so far shown no concern for her fellow students had wanted to help clean up when one of them was sick. If Sheila was ready to help Nellie this way, perhaps the other children were ready to help their classmates in other ways.

On Monday, I thought, we would try something new. Now that Debra and Sheila, who had been the least concerned about others until now, were showing willingness to help others, it was time to start the whole class on a "tutoring" routine. The more advanced readers would help those who were not as far along. This system would give the child who was behind more practice, and it would reinforce the vocabulary of the "tutor." Each student would gain more confidence, and the class as a whole would gain another reading period.

Nellie returned from the washroom with her amiable smile firmly in place. Her momentary upset was forgotten. The classroom was cleaned up again, and we all left the room together.

As the school door was closing after them, I heard the first balloon pop.

Monday, we learned that Kevin had had a surprise of his own over the weekend. He told us about it while the children had their breakfast.

"My Momma come home, an' she bring me a baby sister an' a new Daddy, too," he announced with pride.

"An' I has to mine my sister cause Gramma is poorly." He was obviously filled with a new feeling of importance.

It was delightful to see him so involved with a family of his own. Maybe now there would be enough love in his home for him to feel more secure, and the new security would be reflected in his school work. If all the time he spent daydreaming was spent studying, Kevin might really move forward.

Our morning story was all about Kevin's new family. His sister, he said, was one and a half years old. He said he had not seen his mother for two years. She had told him that was because she was getting his sister, Carrie. In the classroom, Kevin had been referring to his grandmother alternately as "Momma" and "Gramma." The memory of his real mother had obviously become faint until now. Kevin left happily after school to go home to his family. He was happier than I had ever seen him that Monday afternoon.

When the line of children filed into the classroom on Tuesday morning, there appeared to be a stranger in the line. The right side of Kevin's face was distorted beyond recognition. Seeing him from his right side as he entered the room, I did not recognize him. His right eye was swollen almost completely shut, and his face was badly swollen and discolored, too. His brief spurt of animation was gone.

"What happened to you, Kevin?" Looking at him left me feeling physically shaken.

"I forgot to mine my sister an' she fell down an' hurt hersef," he said. "Daddy mad, an' he hit me hard upside my head. Daddy, he leavin' town today, an he doan wan' me forgettin' to mine Carrie while he gone."

All of this was said with sorrow but with no apparent bitterness. Kevin had not felt good about himself before this. Now, it would be almost impossible to build up his self-confidence. He seemed to feel he deserved this type of beating. He had not done the job he had been told to do, so he felt it must be his fault he was punished that severely.

The only good news was that Daddy was leaving town. Hopefully, Daddy would be gone for a long time, if this was his way of training a young child to take care of a new sister.

Breakfast time was unusually quiet that morning. The children digested Kevin's punishment with their cereal. Their quiet deportment indicated they were feeling some compassion for Kevin. His insecurity threatened them all.

There was no morning story for the day until, after some urging, Debra decided to tell us about her big sister, and the way they had played school together over the weekend. According to Debra, this sister was the one who braided Debra's hair into those wonderful pigtails every morning. She also was in charge of seeing to it that Debra was washed and dressed neatly. She did an excellent job of it.

Debra's tale distracted the children from Kevin's punishment and relieved the tension somewhat. The story about Debra's sister, dutifully written on the chalkboard, turned their thoughts to schoolwork.

They all began to copy the story from the board, except for Johnny. He just sat at his desk with an unhappy expression on his face.

"Johnny, why aren't you working?" I wondered if he was still upset by Kevin's swollen face.

"I done lost my pencil," he said softly, as if expecting to be punished.

Two Steps Forward 63

Trying to lighten the atmosphere of gloom, I quipped, "Well, ask, and you shall receive."

"Teacher, tha's from the Bible," he said with surprise.

What unusual children there were in this class: an eight-year-old mentally handicapped child who recognized a quote from the Bible, a seven-year-old mentally handicapped child who was suddenly expected to be responsible for a sister who was just a toddler, plus an eight-year-old mentally handicapped child who was totally responsible for her six-year-old mentally handicapped sister!

In addition, from what they told me, I found that all of the children except Debra, Fred, and Nellie, were sent to the store to buy the family groceries. This was the practice although their math ability was quite insufficient. Only Norman was really able to handle this type of job, and only to a limited degree. The others would not know what they should be charged or what change they should receive. Their practical responsibilities and knowledge were frequently a surprise, though.

Since they were accustomed to handling money, I brought individual bags of pennies to school to help them with their math. The pennies were concrete, a real part of their lives in a way that numerical symbols weren't. They gave meaning to the numbers on the chalkboard or the math papers they were given. They could see the results of their addition and subtraction.

The bags, each with a child's name on it, provided another lesson. Most of the children began to recognize the other children's names as they took turns passing out the bags. That was an unanticipated bonus.

Each day the pennies were carefully put back in the bags and returned to my desk drawer. There were never any missing pennies. Two nickels and a dime were added later. The dimes in particular helped the children who were learning to "borrow" in math.

Norman was steadily working far ahead of the others. He didn't need the coins, and except for a few pennies, Nellie, Fred, and Verna didn't, either, because they were still working at the very beginning of math. Each child received the same amount, though, and appeared to enjoy the responsibility of caring for the coins. The importance they felt when handling the money, and knowing they were trusted to do so, was evident.

As I was preparing for the school day one bleak Monday near the middle of November, I noticed that Harvey's cheerful face did not appear over our windowsill as it usually did. Although he came to school early to check on me less often these days, he always checked to make sure I was there on Monday mornings, as if being away for two days over the weekend would make me forget to come back.

When the bell rang and the doors opened, the children rushed in to tell me that Harvey had been hit by a car when he ran out into the street the day before. He was running from another boy with whom he was playing. He had managed to dodge the boy, but not the car.

Sheila, who had been there, told us how Harvey's body

had bounced off the front of the car when it hit him. "He look like he daid, Teacher. He jus' lie there."

I tried to explain what unconsciousness meant, but I couldn't tell whether or not they understood me. I felt a weakness in my knees when I thought of that agile little body being hurled through the air.

The children had seen some men put him on a stretcher and lift him into an ambulance which had taken him to a nearby hospital. That he had been taken to a hospital, by itself, was frightening to them. I told them I knew he would be well taken care of in the hospital, and I would stop and check on his condition after school. I assumed an air of confidence about his well-being to reassure the children. It was more difficult to reassure myself.

They were obviously concerned. Harvey was a friend to each of them and was the blithe spirit of the classroom. His cheerfulness had carried us through many a tense period during my first days in this room, and his warmth had helped bind me to the class as a whole.

During my lunch hour, I tried to find out about Harvey's condition by calling the hospital. Unfortunately, I could find out nothing about him. It was such a large place that I couldn't find anyone to talk to who even knew who Harvey was.

It was a long school day. We spent our free time in the afternoon making get-well cards for me to take to Harvey. As soon as school was over, I drove to the hospital with the cards.

The hospital was a mammoth, gloomy structure, dressed in city soot and bulging over several square blocks. I walked the equivalent of the perimeter of the building, through halls washed in institutional green, until I finally found Harvey's room. I peeked in with trepidation.

He was lying quietly, a slight figure taking up a disproportionately small space in the big white bed. His cap of black curly hair was a stark contrast to the white pillow. This large, foreign world could swallow him up without his ever being noticed.

He turned and saw me in the doorway and immediately sat up and smiled. His effervescent spirit completely filled the room, and I felt some hope that he was all right. Because he had been knocked unconscious, I had been doubly afraid he might have suffered a head injury which would cause him more learning problems. He didn't need any more problems.

The get-well cards were presented to him, and I helped him decipher the signatures he was unable to read. When they were taken care of, I asked him if he was anxious to get out of the hospital and go home.

"Oh, no, Teacher. They give us CHICKEN here," he said with conspiratorial fervor.

It was a reminder of the eggs he had hungered for, before they had become a frequent item in the classroom. How much larger might he have grown with an adequate diet, and how much had his learning ability been affected by his inadequate diet?

Harvey thought the hospital was a wonderful spot! It was frightening to think he might feel tempted to accost another car, to merit another visit to this land of eggs and chicken. The rest of my visit was spent trying to make sure he knew he was fortunate not to have been badly hurt.

As I was leaving, I saw a nurse nearby and asked her about Harvey's injuries.

"The doctor thinks he's just fine now, but he kept him for observation to be sure there were no problems. He had a slight concussion, you know, but he was unconscious for only a brief time. Besides that, he just has a few bruises from the accident. He seems to feel right at home here in the hospital." Her broad smile said she enjoyed his vivacity, too.

My concern about his being frightened in this foreign place was quite unnecessary. An inability to adapt to new places and new people was definitely not one of Harvey's problems.

The following day, Harvey was welcomed back to the classroom. He had been released from the hospital early that morning and had come to school immediately. It probably would have been better for him to stay home for a day, but here he was. He was a little late. We had finished our breakfast period, but he proudly reassured us that he had had his breakfast in the hospital.

Everyone was delighted to have him back in school. He was treated like, and played the role of, a conquering hero returning from an alien land. And hospitals actually were alien lands to these children. They feared all hospitals. By the time some of their relatives had gone to a hospital, it was too late. To the children, people who went to the hospital never came back.

∽∞∽

Fred's birthday was on the day of Harvey's return, so Fred became the star for the afternoon. He was very solemn, but he kept his head up and looked at the others instead of peeking shyly at them.

When Johnny put Fred's present from the class on his desk, Fred had to be told to open it before he would touch it. He did smile a little when he saw it. His present was a set of little people. Perhaps they would be used as substitutes for the fingers he talked to so often. Whether or not he really understood what was going on when we sang to him and gave him the cards the children had made for him was a moot question. If he had ever had a birthday party, it must have been many years ago. Too long ago for Fred to remember it.

Fred, at ten years of age, was now eligible for the intermediate EMH class. That class still had its quota of children, though, and it was fortunate for Fred that it did. He was just beginning to respond a little to this classroom situation, and it was better not to force another adjustment on him so soon. It would have been a particularly hard adjustment, too, because the intermediate teacher had a slight hearing problem and so often spoke in an unnaturally loud voice. Her voice had a strident quality that penetrated our thin walls and caused the children to feel uneasy at times, although I told them that a loud voice did not always mean someone was angry, as it didn't in this case. The older children knew that the class next door was their next step up on the educational ladder.

During Fred's party, a note came from the office. It stated that we would be receiving a new class member the following day. This time, the student's records had preceded him. Norman's records still had not come. The new student's records hinted that another challenge was about to be presented to the class. They contained a long list of discipline problems caused by the student described. Among them were incidents of petty theft, of attacking other students, and of screaming tantrums.

The academic part of the records noted that the student had developed very few reading skills and was working at a first grade level in math. He had just been moved from a third grade class to an EMH room in another school. Now his family was moving into our area.

The progress the children in this classroom had made would now be tested. They had not had much time to make their improved behavior and more serious attempts to learn a firm part of their characters. In fact, a few, such as Sheila and Kevin, had made very little progress in really trying to learn. The disruption that was sure to come was a real threat to us.

V

ONE STEP BACK

Our new student, Donald, swaggered into the classroom just as a teen-ager might, all his finger-snapping bravado in place. He wore a pixy-like grin as he looked over the class. He then lifted his shoulders and squared them, and his look declared he would take over the group then and there.

He arrived a little late, but the children were still having breakfast. He was invited to have some, too. He was definitely delighted with breakfast, but after it was finished, he had a difficult time settling down to any type of schoolwork. He was loquacious about his likes and dislikes, and his facial expressions amply reflected his opinions. His ready grin was quickly replaced by a scowl when reading was mentioned.

Donald had been using a first grade reader in his previous school. According to his records, his reading ability should fit into the same range as Debra's, Sheila's, and William's.

Norman had shown complete mastery of the first reader and had surged ahead of the other three. He was reading competently in the second reader, now, well ahead of the rest of the class.

When Donald was given the first grade reader, he shoved it away saying, "I'm not gonna read that baby stuff! I can read hard books!"

He didn't seem to realize that I would receive records giving me his reading level in his previous school. Telling him we were reviewing the book and each student could move ahead as quickly as he was able to, brought no response. It was difficult even to make eye contact with him except when he turned on his elfin grin in an effort to manipulate me. His actions were so similar to Sam's that it was disconcerting. I began to wonder how we could get Donald to blend in with the rest of the class.

The other children moved around in the classroom freely now, whenever necessary, without abusing the privilege too often. Donald was unable to handle that freedom. He picked a fight with Johnny before the morning was over and had to be physically restrained from shoving Johnny around the room. Talking to him proved futile. He was intent upon establishing this room as his domain, and he had created a palpable atmosphere of threat.

With Sam gone, Johnny was the tallest boy in the class, except for Fred, who had strategically withdrawn underneath his desk shortly after Donald's arrival. Unfortunately, Johnny's lack of coordination and confidence was apparent for Donald to see, so Johnny became his first target; but Donald's actions threatened the other children as well. They learned to avoid the area around Donald's desk after two of them tripped over his quickly extended foot. Avoiding him in general was something they learned rapidly.

All the turmoil Donald created kept the emphasis off his reading ability, which was probably just what he wanted. No one could see his weakness if he would not read aloud to me. We struggled through the morning with distinct undertones of tension, barely having enough time for the others to read, while Donald pretended to read our library books.

After lunch, Donald was amazed to see that some of the children had bags of real coins to help them with their math. He quickly complained that he couldn't do his math problems without money. He received the bag of coins that Norman no longer took to his seat for math. It worked. The lesson was peaceful until it was time to return the coins.

He watched with disbelief as the other children returned their little bags of money. He refused to give his back. When I walked over to his desk to pick it up, he slammed his body back in his chair and flung the coins across the room. He also flung a few words that didn't belong in the classroom. The other children "ooo-ooohed" and then scurried to pick up the coins for me. I hoped they wouldn't pick up his vocabulary, too.

We had our usual talk about classroom behavior and the rights of others. It seemed a weak response to his actions, but anger or more violence would only beget more of the same. Repetition and example would do more good, I hoped, although it was a slow way to modify the type of behavior Donald demonstrated. I begrudged the time it would steal from the rest of the class, and hoped he would improve before his example encouraged the other children to regress. In comparison, they were all paragons of virtue that day.

After recess, the children came in with horror stories of what Donald had done on the playground. Apparently, he wanted the whole building to know he had arrived in our world. He had shoved and bullied those who were less aggressive. The playground supervisor's patience had been severely tried by his behavior, and she had been about to bring him in to me when the bell rang. I knew I would hear from her later. Indeed, I did hear from her that day, and again, and again, in days to come. Donald finally was threatened with no recess at all, which served to modify his behavior fairly well, although he still managed slyly to go just as far as he could without being sent back to the classroom.

Donald looked somewhat smug about the sensation he had created on his first day with us. I again began the refrain about the benefits of kindness to others, and that making friends was more fun than fighting.

Normally, the children read to themselves for a while after recess, but today I let them all draw to make the day a little easier for them. Art was quickly over when I paused to look at Donald's drawing which he was attempting to show the others. It took a minute for the drawing to register on me. Apparently, Donald had taken an advanced course in anatomy. Perhaps he was more intelligent than the psychologist's test indicated. He did have an eye for detail.

I switched to reading to the class to distract them from Donald's art work. They sat in a semicircle around me, on chairs they had brought up from their desks. While I was reading, Donald danced around the room, made comments about dumb stories, and tossed any loose objects that were left on desks to the floor.

Fortunately, the rest of the class now enjoyed being read to and soon paid only minimal attention to Donald. He began to lose steam. I had chosen several of the children's favorite books so that they could contribute part of the story or could say the rhyming words in the story. They knew them well from previous readings. Finally, Donald came closer to the group. He sat in an empty desk at the edge of the circle. The others were so engrossed in the stories that they ignored his comments. With no audience left, he subsided and began to listen.

We managed to finish his first day in a precarious state of peace.

The children entered in a clump the following morning, vying for position to get through the doorway first. They urged me to look at Fred's hand. Fred showed absolutely no feeling at all as he held up the palm of his hand for me to see. Tiny pieces of tar and bits of gravel were embedded in the scraped flesh, but he acted as if he felt no pain. I cleaned his palm, put on an antiseptic, and two of those wonderful badges of honor for children—Band-Aids.

It was Friday, milk money day. Apparently, Donald had tripped Fred and pushed him down on the playground. He had demanded Fred's milk money. Only the bell ringing and school doors opening had rescued Fred.

Neither the children in our room nor the children in the other classrooms had ever bothered Fred. Perhaps his bizarre behavior or his lack of cleanliness had kept those who were apt to be predaceous at bay. Lately, though, the smell of urine had become less pungent, and he now walked and acted a little more like the other children. His loose, disjointed walk had tightened up. He even said an occasional word or two to the other children instead of talking exclusively to himself. It would not help for him to become a target for the more aggressive Donald. I even silently hoped he had not been better off when left in his own world of make-believe, as he had been in the early fall.

When Donald was asked to apologize to Fred, his response was to use a word that made Debra's "honky" seem tame. The class "ooo-ooohed" for what seemed the hundreth time in the twenty-four hours since Donald joined us.

The other children's attitudes were obviously disparaging toward Donald's behavior. His arrival had caused them to finally coalesce into a group, and form a circle of concern for each other. He was closed out of the circle.

Unfortunately, his actions caused them to be leery of him, and their nervous apprehension was causing them to lose valuable class time. It was difficult for them to concentrate on schoolwork while keeping one eye on Donald. It was difficult for me to concentrate on their lessons and keep one eye on Donald!

My lecture about being kind to each other brought no sign of feeling from Donald. If he had any conception of the pain he caused others, he didn't show it. He was so quick to hit or hurt others in some manner that he was given a wide berth. The children silently edged away when he came toward them.

His desk was quickly moved to the spot next to mine, where Sam's had been. When I put my hand on his shoulder and talked to him quietly about his run-in with Fred, he didn't jerk away as quickly as he had the day before. The physical contact seemed to help him relax, and some of the tension left his wiry body, but he was getting attention for all of the wrong reasons. A way of giving him attention for more positive reasons had to be found as quickly as possible. The progress the class as a whole had made in these past weeks toward a peaceful working atmosphere, was being jeopardized.

Suddenly, the roguish smile reappeared on Donald's face. "Okay, I'm sorry I pushed Crazy Fred. Now can we have breakfast?"

The reason for his changed attitude was not very subtle, but at least there was something that could move him to improve for awhile. We had only minor skirmishes for the rest of the day. His mood swings were wide and frequent, like a constantly moving pendulum.

On his second day with us, Donald read the first reader when the others who were working in it read. It wasn't a reading lesson. He ignored any corrections from me, but at least he was reading. He read with the air of a person performing a tedious task to satisfy some ridiculous expectation of his teacher, bored but determined to humor me and get it over with. He stumbled over many of the words and skipped some he didn't know, but at this first trial he did not seem to have any discernible perceptual problems.

At that time, there were, and perhaps there still are now, some primary teachers who did not feel they needed to require oral reading, but I was not one of them. It took much more time than silent reading, but it was essential for me to hear the children reading out loud to help me understand the types of learning problems each child was having, and to note them immediately. Hopefully, in that way, errors would not be reinforced for too long before I knew about them. It was much easier to correct a problem before it became a firmly ingrained habit. The children did need and did have time for reading alone, too, in order to add to their personal pleasure in reading.

Donald read with no apparent comprehension. He read carelessly, without showing any interest in the content of the reading material. He was a "word caller" and he showed no desire to improve his reading ability. Whether or not he lacked confidence in his ability and was afraid of criticism, so wouldn't make an effort to do well, I could not tell at this time. Admittedly, the book was uninspiring, but Donald's performance when reading it was extreme in its indifference.

The other class members remained angelic through Donald's second day. They looked as though they had always been model students. They were showing this newcomer how to behave! Hopefully, the new leaf they had turned over would not wither too quickly.

Accordingly, on Monday, when Donald was absent, I praised the class for their behavior and asked them to continue to help me by showing Donald how to act in class. Their example was more important than anything I could say to him. They could show him how to be kind to each other and how to work hard in order to learn.

What a heady experience it was for some of them to be models of decorum and scholarship! To see her disdain for Donald's remarks to others, one would never think Debra had a tongue like a knife. Sheila's shrieks diminished, and Harvey stayed put for longer periods of time. Kevin still daydreamed, but he whined less often, apparently not wanting to draw Donald's attention to himself. Fred had to be watched more carefully, however, for he longed for the security of his under the desk-cave. The rest of the class was timid and watchful.

As the days passed, some progress was made in changing Donald's behavior for the better, only to have another hostile scene disrupt our peace. Unfortunately, he was absent far too often, and whenever he returned to school after being absent a day, he was more obviously hostile than before. Our days had a rather erratic pattern, some fairly calm days followed by confrontations or violence. Donald was always more difficult to manage on Mondays, after having been home on the weekend. Talking to him ahead of time in an attempt to avert trouble proved ineffectual. It was as if something at home irritated him powerfully, and when he returned to school, he passed his discomfort onto the other children.

One day, the children came to school with a true horror story. In William's building, there was a woman in a ground floor apartment who served meals in her home to augment her income. William was having dinner with his mother in this apartment the night before when an unknown man came into the room. According to William, he shot and killed the woman who served the meals, turned, and walked out. All of this had happened without a word being spoken.

Donald and Sheila were playing on the sidewalk in front of the building and heard the shots. By the time the police and ambulance came, all the children except Nellie, Nora, and Fred were out in front of the apartment. They all watched as the body was taken away.

Donald had wormed his way close enough to see in a window, and was full of gory details. William, who was actually in the same room with the victim, said very little, but he asked, "Why would anyone want to do such a bad thing?"

We talked about self-control and how our actions sometimes affect other people that we don't even know. It was clear that helping them learn to live successfully in their own environment had to be a part of their primary education. It was difficult for them to build a bridge between the school and their neighborhood. They led double lives, one life as children fairly sheltered in school, and one life as necessarily street-wise semi-adults in their after school hours. They had to protect themselves from all of the intermittent violence they saw and yet learn there were other ways to live.

The violence shook all of them, but Donald reflected the violence that had been so close to him. He jumped up several times to demonstrate the karate kick he would use to retaliate if someone came up to him with a gun. His agitation was difficult to contain. When the subject was changed, he continued to burst forth with other ideas concerning violence.

Since their minds were filled with the murder, we finally used it for their morning writing story. Donald, after having been included in composing the story, didn't seem to notice that his wilder suggestions were left out. He must have felt some satisfaction with the story, since he gradually subsided and did his writing paper, too.

The children wrote, "Our neighbor is gone. A bad man shot her. We are sorry."

It seemed tragic for the shooting to be their written work for the day, but it certainly had more to do with their lives than Spot's bath. There should be some happy medium somewhere for reading and writing materials in less peaceful living areas. Talking about getting along with others in order to increase their awareness of the ramifications of each individual's actions was the only good that could come from this tragedy.

Apparently, talking about kindness did not help Donald. After lunch, when I was helping Nellie and Fred get started with their simple math problems, Donald leaned over to my desk and grabbed one of our goldfish, throwing it to the floor. The usual "ooo-oooh" alerted me, and I put the poor fish back as quickly as possible, but it didn't survive.

Donald had inflicted the violence he had been exposed to on the first available target. It was unfortunate that he was so near the crime. None of the children should have had something like that happen so near to them, but he was the most vulnerable to suggestion.

When the children were leaving school that day, I detained Donald at the door and talked to him again about hurting other people and pets and how much more fun it was to make others feel good. He fidgeted, but something must have gotten through to him because he mumbled,

"Sometime I know not to do somethin' but I jus' go 'head an' do it."

Our talk had to be brief because all the children had to go straight home after school. When the school door closed behind them, they were leaves blown by the wind, scattering swiftly back to their homes. Most of them had to remain inside their homes, if their parents were working, or very close to it, even if an adult was in the home.

The streets and playgrounds were erased of all children in less than an hour after the schools closed because of the gangs who might be about, preying on or trying to conscript their younger neighbors. It was a rare parent who allowed his or her children to be very far from home in the late afternoon or in the evening.

In the summer, some of the parents who could sent their older boys to relatives who lived out of the city. In this manner, they sought to protect their children from the gangs, whose recruitment drives and other activities increased in the spring and summer.

For the more carefully guarded children, school time was their main time to play and frequently the only time they could socialize with their peers. No wonder they wanted to play in class when they began to go to school! The happy days of childhood were not frequent here.

VI

SUCCESSES GREAT AND SMALL

Although the rest of the class was periodically distracted by Donald, nine-year-old Norman had worked on with grim intensity. He worked in his own world within our world. He had left Debra, William, and Sheila behind in reading some time ago. He was able to concentrate on his own work when the less able children were picking out the letters in the alphabet or making the sounds of the consonants. I finally became confident that he was comfortable working at fourth grade math, and we had begun to use a new workbook for it. Now the day had come when he had earned the third grade reader.

He read with confidence and understanding, but until this time, no reading tests had shown his real ability. The word "test" was such a threatening sound to these children who were so unsure of themselves. They were convinced they couldn't do well in a testing situation, and therefore they didn't test well.

Norman became so nervous when faced with a test that almost all thought processes had left him. Answers that he knew well were abruptly forgotten. I began writing simple tests for him, tests that would ensure his achieving success, and gave him two a week. As he began to take the tests more easily, I increased their length and difficulty; finally, I switched to standard tests.

The tests became so routine that Norman relaxed and began to score closer to the norm. The test results were now a little below his apparent ability, but he was on the verge of mastering the testing process. Learning effective methods of test taking was as important as other areas of learning to many of these students, and developing self-confidence was the greatest aide to mastering test taking.

When I announced that Norman was getting a third grade reader, the whole class, with the exception of Donald, clapped. Nellie, Verna, and Fred probably didn't know the significance of Norman getting a third grade reader, but they knew it was something good for Norman. It was heartening to see the children show so much interest in someone else, particularly because they were encouraging Norman who had been so aloof. He had just begun to unbend a little and respond to the friendly gestures of the others. Their cheer of approbation brought the first full smile to Norman's face that I had seen.

Since he was having no real problem in math and was working at the beginning of the fourth grade level almost where he should be and where many of the fourth graders in this school were working, I began sounding out fourth grade teachers about letting Norman join their class for their math period. He was perfectly capable of working in a regular classroom. He would gain confidence from this contact, and it would ensure that he covered the same material the rest of the fourth graders covered. Since it would be only for a limited time each day, it shouldn't be too much of a strain for him, or for the other teacher who would be involved.

My request met with a notable lack of enthusiasm. The low number of students in the EMH classrooms made them appear, to many teachers, an easier place to teach than their own classrooms with larger memberships. Taking a child from such a small class and adding him to their larger class seemed to them to be a burden, even for a short period of the day.

One teacher commented that, with the low number of children in an EMH room, no child from it should have to go to another classroom for any lesson. Those classes, she said, were supposed to be self-contained. She ignored the new confidence it would give Norman and the fact that it would help him adjust to being in a regular classroom again someday. Since I had never taught fourth grade math before and wanted to be sure that Norman had an adequate grounding in it, and since I felt he needed the contact with a regular classroom, I persevered.

Teaching the EMH class made me feel somewhat isolated, as if I had caught some dread disease that wasn't socially acceptable or as if I wasn't quite bright enough to teach average children. This must be the way the children felt, only to a greater degree. When the school day ended, they still carried the terrible stigma of being "different" home with them.

EMH classes were the ones where full-time substitutes were placed if they could be found when there was a shortage of regular teachers. These classes were commonly regarded by regular classroom teachers as an easy spot to be in because of the smaller number of children and because some teachers thought much less should be expected of the students. My main duty, to those with this theory, was to keep the children quiet. These teachers, who had not taught mentally handicapped children, did not always have a full realization of how much the children could learn with enough repetition and varied approaches to learning. They could learn more than how to keep silent.

Silence was not as important to me, except when the noise bothered other children who were trying to learn quietly. It was more important that the children learn than that they remain quiet. We played games to learn whenever they could be devised. From the games the children learned two things: the subject involved and that learning was fun. They did learn in this way, but because it was fun, occasionally their enthusiasm made them too noisy. Even when these children, who had more difficulty learning than most, were achieving in this manner, some teachers, who regarded quiet as the greatest attribute of a "good" class thought the children were undisciplined.

It was more important to me that the children would learn self-discipline instead of an exteriorly imposed discipline that would disappear as soon as they left the disciplinarian's jurisdiction or became old enough to challenge the teacher's discipline. Helping the children learn self-discipline might lessen the incidents of children in the upper grades overwhelming teachers and taking over the classes themselves. With patience, these children could be taught that they would be the ones to benefit from practicing self-discipline.

The unfortunate teachers, usually substitutes or beginning teachers, who encountered children who had never learned self-discipline and children who had been repressed constantly, reaped what had been sown during the children's earlier years. Too often, these teachers left the teaching field rapidly when they could have become contributing members of the teaching profession under different circumstances.

In the disciplinarian's classroom, when the children tried to socialize a little, a battleground atmosphere emerged. A continuing power struggle followed, until the teacher's will prevailed. Then, some of the children became withdrawn, timid, hostile, or truant—retarded by discipline or fear.

There were many teachers in this school who were not this rigid—teachers who managed to have control in their classes without crushing the spirits of the children or by making the children feel stupid or rejected. Those teachers were gifted in fostering an enthusiastic but well-behaved class in which the children were comfortable but still learned. The children in these classes seemed to learn more rapidly, and no children were disturbed emotionally as a result of the classroom atmosphere. At the end of each year, when it had been time for my children to move up the educational ladder, I always hoped the children from my class would get this type of effective teacher the next year, a teacher who wasn't threatened by a child's enthusiasm.

One such teacher did agree to try Norman in her math class. She did not complain about having an extra student to teach but was more concerned about whether or not Norman could achieve at the same pace her children maintained. She was also concerned because she had heard that he was a discipline problem.

Norman, with his studious old gentleman's manner, had never been a discipline problem in our class, even with the prime examples around him. Something had undoubtedly happened at some time in his previous school, but it simply did not seem possible for him to have a terrible temper and for him not to have shown it by now in our room.

His records finally arrived at the school. There was nothing in them to substantiate the temper rumor. There was little indication of what level he had been working at, or anything else about him, either. His placement in the EMH class was a puzzle, one that should be solved soon.

His new math teacher and I decided he should start taking math with her after the approaching Christmas holiday was over. She would be reviewing some of the material her class had covered in the fall, before she went on to new material. Since I had not taught this math level before, the review would ensure that he had mastered as much as her class had.

Norman and I began talking about the advantages of his learning math in a fourth grade room, since his math was so far ahead of the others in our room. I told him he had achieved very well here but he needed to be with children who were learning the same things he was. He had to be made comfortable with the thought of changing classes well ahead of time. It would not help him if he were unprepared for the change. He would become nervous and unable to achieve as much as he was capable of because he was placed in an unfamiliar atmosphere without being prepared for it.

Meanwhile, the official forms had been filled in, requesting that Norman be retested for possible full-time placement in a regular classroom again. They had been sent to the psychologist's office at the board of education, where they would await their turn to be considered.

Mentally handicapped children begin to appear more and more normal to a teacher who works with them all the time, but Norman could not possibly be mentally handicapped and work at about his grade level in math and be just a little over a year behind in reading. A year behind in reading level was not uncommon in the regular classrooms. In fact, national statistics indicate that children in large city areas such as this one were sometimes two or more years behind in reading by the sixth grade. These statistics are for children who are still in the regular classroom.

The terrible temper that Norman was reputed to have had never shown up in our class, and I did not expect that it ever would. He did have some quality or reserve about him that kept both Donald, or any of the other aggressive children from other classrooms from challenging him. Whatever that quality was, it was a blessing.

There was nothing in his records to indicate what had caused his previous teacher to have him tested. One person had put him in the testing situation; one test had put him in the mentally handicapped class. It has been noted, statistically, that simple anxiety can cost a test taker seven or eight points on an intelligence test. Norman, with his previous fear of tests, had undoubtedly frozen in the testing situation and had been placed in the EMH class on the basis of that one test.

Now he needed help in adjusting to a return to the regular classroom, even on a part time basis. If he were tested in the near future, with his new self-confidence and the added experience of taking math in the regular class, he would surely be reassigned to a regular class full-time. In the meantime, taking math with the fourth graders would help him bridge the gap from our world to theirs. Some days that looked like a long bridge to cross.

On the day that Norman received his new reader, Donald was absent again. He had been absent far too often since he had joined our class, averaging almost six absentee days a month. The truant officer had spoken to his mother to no avail. She received notes from me, but she had neither responded, nor had she sent him to school more regularly. His records from his previous school indicated that attendance had always been a problem.

When he first began coming to our school, he frequently was tardy, also. The tardiness ended when he found out he missed breakfast when he wasn't on time. No matter how much he cajoled, no matter what tantrums he threw, he received no breakfast when he arrived late. Breakfast, in fact, had turned out to be the best behavior modifier for him so far. It couldn't be given up as such since the reward of breakfast guaranteed his prompt arrival at school.

Since he enjoyed breakfast so much, it was surprising that he was absent so often. Obviously, breakfast was not available at home for him or he wouldn't have been so anxious for it at school, but he still missed school. It was disheartening to see him miss school so often. He was capable of reading in the first grade reader with Debra, William, and Sheila, but when he was put with them, he kept falling behind again and again because of his many absences. Then he would resent having to read stories with vocabulary they had already covered. His math followed the same pattern of alternately catching up and falling behind the others.

William had had the same problem when he was in the first grade, but William had never been belligerent. Now William never missed school, and he was doing very well. Surprisingly, none of the other children, with the exception of Nellie who had been absent for two days with a cold, ever missed school. Their attendance record was amazing.

Some method of improving Donald's attendance would have to be found. Consequently, I asked another teacher who was very interested in helping all of the children to go with me to Donald's house during our lunch hour.

He lived two blocks away, in an apartment building right behind a corner tavern. Nora lived above that tavern, and Fred lived in the building next to it, above still another tavern. No sound came from any of these buildings. In fact, the whole area appeared deserted during this noon hour.

The entry hall of Donald's building smelled as though the tavern goers had used it for a lavatory for many years. It was uncomfortably dark, as were the stairs, letting your imagination project images of what might be in there with you.

Donald's apartment was on the third floor, and I thanked the other teacher again and again for coming with me as we climbed the dark, steep stairs. When we found Donald's apartment at the rear of the building, we heard children's voices on the other side of the door. Our knocking brought no response, and after a spate of whispers, it became quiet inside the apartment.

After knocking several times, without any results, I called out, "Donald, this is your teacher. Please open the door."

The door opened magically. Donald stood there with no trace of his elfin smile.

"I can't come to school cuz I'm minding my sisters. Momma's gone to get her hair done."

Two little girls about four-years-old and three-years-old peeked at us solemnly from behind Donald. A toddler wandered over with nothing on except an undershirt.

The half of the room to the right of the door was almost completely taken up with a double bed mattress, which lay on the floor. A naked baby lay sleeping on it. The left half of the room contained a small table, two wooden chairs next to it, a small stove and refrigerator, and a sink on legs.

Across from the doorway where we stood, there was a doorway to a second room. In that room there were two double bed mattresses, also on the floor, one each on either side of the doorway. Except for a narrow path between them, they completely covered the floor. A small chest was against the far wall between the mattresses. A burning candle stood on the chest. There was a narrow window in the left wall of each room.

The entire apartment was within our view. There was no other space, and there was no bathroom. The urine-gymnasium smell in the room was overpowering. It was easy to understand why Donald shared Fred's odor problem. What a difficult life they must lead, and how much more important that made it for Donald to do well in school!

We left a note for Donald's mother, stressing that Donald not be kept out of school unless he was ill. He was back in school the next day, and his attendance improved dramatically after that visit. Whether it was because we had shown enough interest to visit his mother's home or because she realized the school personnel now knew that she kept an eight-year-old child home to babysit while she had her hair done didn't matter. What did matter was that Donald had benefited from our visit.

He was now able to keep up with Sheila easily. Debra and William moved ahead of them in the reading book. Debra now openly showed that she dearly loved to read, and William worked diligently to keep up with her. They were over halfway through the first reader. Some of the new vocabulary in this reader had evidently been in some of the other books that had crossed their paths, because they were retaining it fairly easily.

Our "tutoring" system was firmly established and was working well, for the most part. Donald had Norman for his reading helper because Norman's reserve kept Donald from challenging him or, more importantly, from trying to provoke him. Agitation was still Donald's favorite sport. I also chose Norman to help Donald because he had more patience. The "tutoring" helped build up Norman's confidence and reinforced his reading vocabulary, while it helped increase Donald's reading ability.

Since she and Donald were at the same level, Sheila joined Norman and him now. She was doing fairly well but had still not developed a real desire to learn, and she did not retain new vocabulary as well as some of the others did. Even having William and Debra move ahead of her had not increased her desire to keep up. She was not as competitive about her reading as she was about so many other things. She needed constant encouragement. It seemed impossible to find a good motivation to use with her.

We now had two short reading periods during which the children helped each other with their reading or read quietly to themselves. These periods were in addition to our main reading period, when I worked with them singly or in pairs.

Sheila always wasted the period during which she was supposedly reading to herself, so one day I asked her to help Kevin during that time. She loved it! It satisfied her naturally bossy nature, and she prodded Kevin relentlessly. She became more interested in mastering the vocabulary herself, lest she lose her powerful new position as tutor. It was the best solution to her lack of motivation that could have been found, and it was just what Kevin needed, too.

Never did a mother hen cluck at a chick more than Sheila did at Kevin. It was not as peaceful a process as it could have been, and I might have given it up in despair at the added noise except that it was working! Kevin had someone else to give him an extra needed push. He also had someone else to brag about him if he did progress, and another person to whom he was very important. He was responding to this additional attention.

Without Sheila's or my proddings, Kevin had shown little interest in learning. His mother had left their home again, leaving Kevin's little sister behind for Kevin and his grandmother to care for. After she left, he spent days in a dream world. His body was here, but his mind did not want to come to terms with his life and floated somewhere out of my reach.

When he began to function again, he wasn't quite as babyish as he had been, and he didn't whine as much. He had grown more quiet and was more distant from the others; he was no longer trying to make new friends. He now had a younger sibling for whom he was responsible, at least for part of the time, but the extra family member didn't help him. He was still such an unhappy child that he was unable to leave his problems and worries at home.

Since Kevin had developed no interest in learning on his own, he had to be bribed or pushed every inch of the way. With Sheila pushing and me bribing, we began to make some progress. Teaching a passive, indifferent child took at least the same amount of effort as teaching two or three children who were anxious to learn. Sheila had a vast amount of energy, and this was a good outlet for it.

The tutoring system was another way to provide the extra amount of repetition needed for the majority of the children in this class. Debra helped Annabelle, without any of her previous cutting remarks, and William helped Johnny. In their groupings, all of their disparate needs were met as well as possible.

Although I was available, when needed, to help anyone with a difficult word, the greater part of these periods was spent helping Harvey and Nora. Because they each had perceptual problems, they needed additional individual help. It was difficult for them to do the work put on the chalkboard for the rest of the class. Even though we folded the papers to form squares corresponding to the number of problems on the board, they tended to leave out numbers or to put them in the wrong places on their papers, making a puzzle out of a group of simple math problems. They could do the problems verbally or when they were printed on paper for them, but they often had difficulty copying them and putting the answer in the proper place.

Writing their morning story was very difficult for them, and it took them much longer than it took the others to do these short assignments. Their eyes refused to shift from the board to their paper, and to keep their writing on a straight line was impossible.

When reading, these two tended to reverse words or leave them out entirely, sometimes skipping to the line below in the middle of a line, and leaving out half a line of print. The sentence they were reading then wouldn't make sense, and they would have to go back to the beginning to find the meaning in what they read. This process tired and frustrated them, but with help I hoped they would outgrow the problem. A piece of paper held under the line they were reading did help, although I knew it was a frowned-on practice. It was important to keep their confidence intact and their will to succeed as strong as possible until learning could be more easily accomplished.

It was not too difficult to keep Harvey's spirit intact because he surprisingly always had his own joy of life. He also wanted everyone around him to be happy, so he cheerfully encouraged Nora to keep trying when she became discouraged, even though his problems were much more severe than hers were.

One day, the children had been particularly studious and cooperative, so we decided to go to the bakery for a reward. Our trips to the bakery had become a regular reward system, since they also augmented our breakfast. Now that Donald had joined the class, the trips were not as pleasant. Donald's disruptive behavior had begun to reinfect the other children. Some of the bickering and shoving when in line had returned to unsettle us on our walks, so we had not been going once a week as we had before he joined the class.

The woman who worked in the bakery had initially viewed our visits with dismay. As the children had become more orderly and our visits had become a regular event, she gradually grew more friendly. She had even begun talking to one or the other of the children. The children had responded well to her, since she was the dispenser of good things.

Donald's first visit ended all of our hard won rapport with her, however. He tried to snatch a package of cupcakes, and when restrained, he thrashed around struggling to free himself from my grasp. My theories on tolerance and encouraging self-discipline wavered momentarily. The fabric of our patiently woven decorum began to unravel.

The bakery lady retreated again, her face taut, her counter a barricade. I threatened to eliminate all our walks, even those to the main school for assemblies. The threat slowed Donald down, although still on subsequent walks when we arrived at our destination in an orderly fashion, we too often returned to the annex in a helter-skelter manner. Nevertheless, we continued the short trips as practice for a longer one.

Before Donald had transferred into our class, we had talked about taking a field trip to the local zoo when the children had earned it by learning to walk together as they should all of the time. They needed so much more exposure to the larger community out there. They needed the sights, the sounds, and the smells that were common to other children.

The trip would be a growing experience for all of them, and it was unfair to deny all of the children this experience, or any other experience, because of one renegade. Although I knew it would be unfair to ask another teacher to keep him for a day, the possibility of Donald remaining behind was mentioned to him. A zoo trip was now held as a carrot on a stick in front of Donald each time we left the building. It achieved its purpose only part of the time.

Donald promised to try harder each time we set out, but the stimulus of being out in the world, seeing different places and different sights, would often be more than he could handle, and he would revert to his disruptive behavior. We always set out with each of the children having different partners each trip, but before we could get back to our room, Donald would be the one forced to walk with the teacher. Asking Donald to behave in an orderly manner was like asking the bubbles in a carbonated drink to stay at the bottom of the glass.

When we returned to the annex from the bakery that particular day, we found an apparently drunken man passed out near the school. His body lay across the sidewalk leading to the entrance of the annex.

Two teen-agers who should have been in school were going through his pockets. A third teen-ager was examining his wallet. When I called to them, they began to run away. I called to them again. The boy who held the wallet threw it back toward me. It was empty, of course, and I gingerly tucked it under the man's outstretched arm. Donald grinned at the departing teen-agers as if seeing kindred spirits.

The presence of the unfortunate man did not seem to surprise the children at all. A few of them giggled at him, and the rest of them ignored him. He was not an unusual sight to most of them. He was just the opposite of the adult image they most needed in their lives.

Good role models for the children were not always easy to find, either in teenagers or adults.

VII

OUT IN THE REAL WORLD

One morning Harvey shinned up to our classroom window to show me his new winter coat. "Saturday, Momma gimme four dollars," he said. "She tole me to go to the resale store an' buy myself a new coat for the winter."

"What a nice coat, Harvey. You certainly did a good job picking such a good, warm one." He glowed with satisfaction at his success.

He had walked ten blocks, through an unknown area. Passing through an unknown neighborhood was almost never done here. It was considered very dangerous. He had crossed a very busy intersection to reach the store. There he found himself a coat that was good and warm for his four dollars. He bought it all by himself. It was a blue wool sailor-style coat with a slightly lumpy, but heavy, lining. It was clean, and it was warm. He was quite proud of his purchase, and he deserved to be.

This was quite an accomplishment for a boy of eight who was labeled mentally handicapped. It made me wonder again whether or not all the facets of intelligence were being measured in the standard intelligence tests, just as I wondered how accurate they were. How well would an eight-year-old child from a more affluent area do if faced with the task of finding, in an unknown area, the best coat he could buy for four dollars? Certainly Harvey had a perceptual problem that hindered his learning in some ways, but his other abilities did not seem limited at all. He showed an excellent understanding of other people, and a good understanding of what was told to or read to him.

Our morning story for the day centered around Harvey's new purchase. It was a confidence-building story. Although his verbal abilities were more developed than most of the others, Harvey's insecurity showed up when he had a written task to copy. He invariably was up and down for several minutes with time-killing tasks, trying to postpone the moment when he had to work with the pencil and paper. His own story encouraged him to try to write well. Anything that would build confidence for him, or any of the others, was a bonus for our room.

All the other children seemed impressed with Harvey's shopping ability, all except Donald who was openly jealous of the extra attention Harvey was getting. Donald ridiculed the coat Harvey had bought and stated that he could easily go and buy a coat for himself. He was not afraid to walk anywhere.

As Donald's comments became louder and more derogatory, he appeared to be testing Harvey's patience to see how much derision Harvey would take before he retaliated. Perhaps he was testing me as well to see just how far he could go. He knew speaking kindly was the class rule. He had heard it often enough to last a lifetime.

"That a pimp coat," he said. "Nobody wanna coat like that."

My continual repetition of the class rule to speak kindly or not at all, a request that had been made over and over to Debra, when she had muttered insults to others in days past, didn't change his behavior at all. Finally, I stated that anyone who couldn't be kind to his classmates would have to skip breakfast the next day. It was really a reflex action, the type of threat I didn't like to make. But it had to be preferable to letting Donald diminish Harvey's hard earned self-confidence, and to the feeling of hostility that Donald was generating which would harm the whole class. Whether making the threat was right or wrong, it worked, and Donald quieted down for awhile. His favorite part of the day had been put in jeopardy. Bribery can't be all bad.

This was the first time Donald had openly attacked Harvey with such a vengeance. His usual targets were Johnny, Fred, William, Kevin, or one of the more submissive girls, never Debra or Sheila. He had tried Debra once, but her spiteful verbal barrage made him retreat quickly. Debra was a more kind person now, but she had not forgotten all of her old protective devices. Sheila was enough larger and testy enough herself to keep him at bay.

At times, I felt that Donald would like to stop his taunting or physically aggressive behavior and become one of the group, but he just couldn't seem to maintain control of himself. Sometimes, when some of the children were playing or studying companionably, he would look at them as if he wanted to be a part of their circle, but then he would do whatever was the most apt to keep him shut out. If he was being physically aggressive, I would have to escort him to his desk, which I would pull closer to mine.

In the morning when I arrived at school, I always pushed Donald's desk several feet away, but most days, by late afternoon, it would be back next to mine. As the day progressed, and he had less and less control over himself, his desk would be moved forward. It seemed to help him gain some control of his aggressiveness to have someone close by to help him remember to practice some restraint. He told me that sometimes he didn't want to act the way he did, but he just couldn't stop. Typically, the more he needed love and approval, the more difficult he made it for anyone to give them to him. A hand on his shoulder could help him control himself, but eventually he had to learn self-control for the sake of his own survival and happiness, if not for everyone else's. There would not always be someone else there to remind him how to behave.

Our many talks about the rights of others appeared to help until the moment he felt someone else was getting too much attention. Fortunately, he could be praised now for his improved schoolwork, and that helped his behavior. His regular attendance had increased the speed of his progress. He took his turns with the classroom tasks and could be praised for these, also, but he needed still more attention and praise.

The anecdotal record that I kept of his behavior was not too encouraging, but occasionally a note of improvement could be added. We would sometimes have a few peaceful days, and then there would be a drastic setback. I would reread the record then, seeking assurance that we were making progress. We were. His provocative behavior was occurring less frequently now.

It was unfair to penalize the whole class because of Donald's lack of control, so we would have our trip to the zoo before the winter weather could curtail our activities. Each parent was invited, by note, to come along, but Nellie's mother was the only one who replied. She agreed to come with us and help supervise the children.

All the permission slips were signed, and most of the children brought their lunches on the day of the trip. I brought several lunches, knowing some would be forgotten and some would be unobtainable. As expected, Fred, Donald, and Annabelle had no lunch. Verna did not come, either from fear, or perhaps because her mother was concerned about her safety. Annabelle said Verna wasn't sick.

The day of our trip was one of those December days that dressed itself as spring, hiding its cloudy skies and cold wind in a closet somewhere to the north of us. Everyone was excited, smiling, and anxious to go when our big yellow bus pulled up in front of the school. But when we began to climb aboard, Debra began wailing, "I'm not going on that dumb bus. We'll all be killed. You can't make me go."

All the muttered bravado of this little girl had been a defense for a child frightened of the unknown. It took minutes of talking, washing her face, and going to the bathroom again to calm her down. By then, most of the others decided they'd better go to the washroom again, too. Debra's fear was making them nervous. Finally, twenty minutes later, assured she would sit with me, Debra and the other children got on the bus. The driver's look said, "Really, Lady!"

Fortunately, it was not a long ride, because, since I was sitting with Debra, Donald was given more freedom to pester the others who were within his reach. He could not leave his seat because Nellie's mother was sitting on the aisle side of him at my request. Although she had seen Donald during her classroom visits, she was unaccustomed to coping with Donald's erratic behavior, and at a loss as to how to restrain his poking fingers and swinging arms. It was a good thing his curiosity about the sights we were passing engaged his attention often, so he was more of an intermittent aggravation than a serious threat to the others. Still, it was a relief when the bus ride was over.

When we got off the bus, I delegated Debra to Nellie's mother, who now had Nellie on one side and Debra on the other. I took Donald firmly by the hand. Each of the other children had a partner, except for Johnny who could be trusted to stay with us no matter what happened. Accordingly, I asked Johnny to walk at the end of the line and make sure everyone was in line ahead of him whenever we left one animal's exhibit for another. This job made him stand straighter and hold his head higher. In his fringed jacket, he was at least a deputy, if not a marshal, he thought. He was a very important part of our group.

Our weeks of walking together to the bakery or over to the main school for assemblies produced results. The children kept their partners with them and moved in an orderly fashion from one exhibit to another, until we were ready to leave the zebras. There, when I called to Johnny and we started walking, I heard a child cry out in a frightened voice.

Turning back, I saw an extra child in our line. Johnny had spotted a young boy who had wandered from his mother's side. With winter coats and hats on, Johnny had not noticed that the boy was not "ours" and had tried to put this boy in our line. His mother rushed over and jerked him away. She didn't wait for my explanation, and her face expressed her opinion of Johnny's apparent "aggressive behavior." Johnny looked confused. He was unaware that he had taken his duties too seriously, but conscious something was not quite right. Everyone in line meant *everyone* in line to Johnny.

In the days preceding our trip, we had made lists of the animals we most wanted to see. Nellie, Fred, and Verna had cut out pictures of animals from old magazines for each of their classmates to identify. The children named the animals they were able to, and I put each name on a separate piece of construction paper. All of the children then pasted the pictures on the page of construction paper that had the correct name of the animal printed on it. These papers were hung on the bulletin board so the animals and their names would become familiar to those who didn't know them.

When we got to the children's zoo, nothing would convince Annabelle that the baby elephant was really only a baby, so we detoured to find the large elephants. After seeing the full-grown elephants, Annabelle conceded that the babies were truly babies. She also was convinced she did not want to linger around the large elephants. We would have many discussions about sizes and shapes after this day. Comparative words had been given more meaning to them now.

The excitement of seeing all the live animals tired the children, so we stopped for lunch a little early. It was a peaceful moment, and we sat and relaxed at the picnic tables for an extra few minutes to give both the children and the adults a rest.

Even the less verbal children were talking about all we had seen. Harvey's usual delight in life was bubbling out of him as he demonstrated the way the elephants stood, leaning over and using his arms held together as a trunk and then swaying back and forth. Even Donald was more inclined, for awhile, to talk about what we had seen rather than bait the other children. But the lunch and rest were suddenly over when Donald began running around the picnic table, poking different children on each circuit. We decamped in a hurry when Sheila, having been rudely poked, raced after Donald to retaliate.

We continued our tour. Aside from Debra becoming hysterical at the sight of the big bus, Johnny grabbing a strange little boy, and Donald annoying everyone possible, the trip was turning out to be a most successful event. Then we took the children to the restrooms. Once he was inside the men's room, Donald realized I would be unable to come in and get him if he decided to stay in there. The rest of us waited, thinking he would get tired and bored and eventually come out on his own, but he was enjoying his prank. He had no intention of giving up his moments of extra attention.

He would come as far as the door, peek out, then laugh at us and retreat. We tried walking away to see if he would follow us, but I could not take the chance of losing him, so we didn't go very far. It was possible that Norman could physically retrieve him, but I did not want to risk developing any animosity between them. Donald did not come out. Leaving the children with Nellie's mother, I finally went and found a guard. I asked him to go in and bring Donald back to the fold. The guard probably wondered at our lack of discipline.

I tried to keep my dignity by looking extra stern when Donald was, at last, handed over to me by the guard. He was grinning and very pleased with himself. Actually, I was glad that his misbehavior had been in the nature of a prank rather than in some cruelty that caused pain to someone else.

Debra wailed again when she saw the bus waiting for us, but the wail was short-lived. We returned to the school, a tired but happy class. We took with us many ideas for the morning stories the children would create and many mental pictures of the animals and sights we had seen, which they would attempt to draw. It was a big world out there. Several of the children had never been to a zoo, so their horizons had been greatly widened.

Except for a long stay in front of the men's room, we had had a near perfect day.

Soon after our trip, I brought a camera to school and took each child's picture. They didn't really believe that their pictures had been taken until I brought the pictures to school a few days later. Each child feasted his eyes on his own picture. We would have gotten little work done that day if there hadn't been an extra picture for each child, which I promised they could take home after school if they had finished their work. The promise of their own copy induced them to leave the bulletin board where their likenesses were hung long enough to get their schoolwork finished.

The set of pictures on the bulletin board remained there for the rest of the year. The children often paused in front of the board to innocently admire themselves. When we talked about their pictures, we decided that the children on the bulletin board were always kind to each other. We talked about the nice things they said to each other, they never hit or pushed each other. They were good, and they worked hard in school. They were anything we wanted them to be!

Since what you believe children are and what you help them believe they are is frequently what they become, the class in general blossomed. Gradually, the children began to believe all the good things we said about each of them were true. And they were—almost.

A reasonably quiet, productive period followed. It lasted until the Christmas holidays came near. We planned a Christmas party for our classroom. A friend of mine, who had played Santa Claus for my first graders, was coming to hand out the gifts to the children. All the other classes in the annex were planning to have a party, too, and the building throbbed with excitement.

It did not matter that the children said, repeatedly, that there was no Santa Claus. We talked about the spirit of giving, and I tried to explain Santa as a symbol of giving. But when Santa finally did arrive, there was an instant, profound silence in our room. The room had never held such a living, pulsing quiet.

When Santa tried to have some personal talks with the children, even Harvey lost his conversational ability. Santa had always been able to establish rapport quickly with the other children I had taught, but these children were overwhelmed. Only Nellie, who had perhaps seen a Santa Claus more often, would talk a little with him. Santa still managed to find something special to say to each child, and no one in our room ever said there was no Santa Claus again. Just to say such a thing would be like killing the goose that laid the golden egg.

The children had a round-eyed, trancelike look of wonder on their faces when Santa called them, one at a time, to come up to him and receive their presents. Perhaps it was just wonder that someone would give them presents, but the ambience was one of elusive Christmas magic.

Friends had sent so many gifts for them, that each child received at least two appropriate presents. Even Donald was particularly satisfied with a large dump truck he received as one of his presents. There was no bickering or jealousy that day. The children displayed an interest in the gifts their classmates received, but all of them were happy with the presents that were their own.

Since I dreaded the loss in reading vocabulary the children were apt to suffer over the holidays, I gambled and told them that those who wanted to could take their reading books home and practice their reading while school was not in session. I was reluctant to do this because I had had so many warnings in the past about "those" children losing their reading books. The unwritten rule was that no reading books went home with the children. Until now, I had contented myself with letting them take our "library" books home. But now they were more interested in reading and therefore, presumably, more interested in taking care of the books. All the children held onto sturdy bags for their gifts and their reading book when they left for their homes. They carried them out to their world armed with smiles and happy chatter.

As it was to all teachers and students, the holidays and a little rest were enjoyable to me, but when it was time to return to school, I was anxious to see how the children had fared over the holiday. The class was called a special education class. It certainly was a special education for me. And the children were special, too!

VIII

HOLIDAY REWARDS

The first day of school after the holidays became another holiday for all the schoolchildren in the city. Sixteen inches of blowing snow fell the previous night. Radio stations read bulletins issued by the board of education advising all parents to keep their children at home for the day. Since almost all streets were impassable, school buses were unable to transport the children who needed them and walking a few blocks would be difficult or impossible for smaller children.

Many teachers were unable to get to school, and most of the classrooms were empty. It was quite a surprise, then, to see William arrive at school, bundled from head to foot and none the worse for having walked three blocks through the snow to school. Whatever his health had been in the past when he was absent so often, it was certainly excellent now, and when his mother said he would be there every day, she meant *every* day.

William was one of the children who had taken his reading book home over the holidays, and he was eager to tell me that he had read all of it. When he read to me, I was delighted to find that he knew all the vocabulary words; in addition, his comprehension was excellent. He was now ready for a second grade reader. His mother must have had him read to her every night for him to have covered so much material and for him to know it so well. It was doubly satisfying to know they both had an interest in his educational achievements.

He had shown no serious lack of retention in this class, and it did not seem possible to me that this boy was really mentally handicapped, any more than I thought Norman and, perhaps, Debra were. His records indicated that he had been absent as often in his previous school as he had been in this school during the first part of first grade. Unless a child is intellectually well above average and has sufficient help at home, it is impossible for him or her to keep up with children who attend school regularly. William, however, had now gone from excessively absent to compulsively present.

Perhaps he had been too timid to enjoy the hurley-burley of school and all the strangers encountered there during his first two years, and so had coaxed his mother to let him stay home with her. Now, his mother was working and gone from their home all day, so school was preferable to an empty apartment. He thus began to demonstrate how much he could achieve with a serious attempt at schoolwork. He began to mature socially, too, and was more comfortable with his peers, particularly with those who were not unduly aggressive.

In addition to working on some reading and math, we got to know each other better that day. William was a quiet boy, but he became more talkative when he had no one to compete with him for attention. He was quite happy to spend a small part of the day helping me clean and get the classroom ready for the coming months.

"I help my mother, too, when she cleans our house on Saturdays," he confided to me. Then, he became bolder. "You know, Teacher, I din't used to like school when I was little, but now I think it's fun. Reading is okay, too." We shared my lunch and his secret, and we gained a little more understanding of each other.

The next day, when all of the children were back in school, Debra told me she had finished her reading book, also. Her mastery of it was almost as complete as William's was, and she was almost a year younger. She was also ready for a second grade reader, which meant she was only reading six months behind grade level. I wished there were a second grade class in the annex where she could read with her peers. I was very proud of her and, what was more important, she was very proud of herself. She told us that she and her oldest sister had played school every day over the holidays.

Debra had two older sisters. The oldest one helped her with her reading and her grooming. The next oldest sister was in an EMH class. Perhaps the fact that she had an older sibling in an EMH class, plus Debra's hostility when frightened by new experiences or new people, had encouraged someone to have her tested for this class. Teachers' expectations of what children are, or what they can do, often set the pattern for what they will become.

Both she and William would have to be retested. Mentally handicapped children could not master so much vocabulary in just a few short months. It appeared that their minds had been on idle and then had shifted into high gear when they were ready to achieve. I filled out the forms requesting retesting for possible placement in regular classes and sent them to the psychologist's office where Norman's form waited in line, hoping it wouldn't be too long before all three were tested again. Every week was important to them. All the children had lost six weeks at the beginning of the school year, and some of them had lost much more time in previous years.

There was a shortage of school psychologists then, and it was far easier to get placed into an EMH class than to get out of one. Precedence for testing was given to those who had never been tested; that removed children who were difficult to handle or to teach from the regular classroom more quickly. Since that time, a law has been passed requiring that each child who is in a mentally handicapped class be retested every three years. Of course, if a mistake were made in placing a child in an EMH room, waiting three years for reappraisal results in a tremendous loss of time for that student.

Fortunately, the new laws concerning the mentally handicapped have other provisions for maintaining a continuing assessment of each child's abilities and progress. At the time, however, intelligence quotients were generally considered to be more or less static so that, once a child was deemed mentally handicapped, he or she was apt to be considered so permanently. There was not much thought given as to whether or not the student was utilizing all of his or her capabilities in the testing situation, or utilizing them in the classroom. Regard was not always paid to whether or not the psychologist was able to establish rapport with the student before the test. The possibility of a faulty test performance was seldom given serious consideration.

Our breakfast conversation took longer than usual to become a morning story the first day all the children were back in school. Most of the children had something they wanted to talk about, and Donald had come back to school in a highly agitated mood. He didn't like the attention William and Debra were getting for their reading progress, and he talked about nothing except a boy named Tyrone who had moved into his building and was two years older than Donald.

Tyrone was known throughout the school as a bully and troublemaker, but Donald was impressed with Tyrone's power over other children and was enchanted at having him as a friend. He seized every opportunity to tell us about those whom Tyrone had beaten up and about what good friends he and Tyrone were. To Donald, the ability to frighten or irritate another was power, and power made him feel better about himself. It was better to be an annoyance than to be nothing. Luckily, Tyrone's classroom was in the main school building, so we should not have constant reminders of him encouraging Donald in his less desirable behavior on the playground.

It was unfortunate Donald and Tyrone lived in the same building. Donald did not need that type of influence; he was aggressive enough without it and he was soon trying to cause trouble again. Unfortunately what had been forgotten over the holidays was not all academic. We once again began our litany about being kind to each other, not hurting each other, not taking away the learning time of others.

With William and Debra starting the second grade reader, Donald and Sheila were the only ones reading the first grade reader. They were a volatile combination, but Sheila was enough larger than Donald, and was never known to be intimidated, so their battles were verbal rather than physical. Neither one was sure he or she could prevail over the other one physically, and neither wanted to find out who was the stronger the hard way. Also neither one had felt the need to try to keep up with their reading over the holidays, so they were both reviewing what they had forgotten, as were all the children who had not taken books home.

Harvey had taken his book home, but he had lost it. He was not careless, but he did have difficulty keeping track of things. One lost book was well worth the progress William and Debra had made, however.

Johnny, Harvey, Annabelle, Nora, and Kevin were due for a different book after reviewing the old one. They would get another primer from a different series. Unfortunately, this series had no more connection with reality for them than the other series had, but it was what was available. They had finished their old primer, but needed more practice with the same level of vocabulary before they could start a first grade reader. A new book would make them feel that they, too, were making progress, while giving them needed repetition.

Norman began going to the fourth grade classroom for his math lessons and no problems ensued, although he was noticeably tense when he first left us to join them and my attempted use of a little humor to relax him fell flat, as it usually did with Norman. The world was such a serious place for him.

As the weeks went by, he began to relax, and his new math teacher began to like and respect this serious boy. He remained quiet and studious, but he became a little more sociable with the others and he looked happier. After a while, he began to play with the other fourth graders when recess time came.

The language ability of almost all the children was noticeably improved since the fall. Each of them, except Verna and Fred, had told me something about their holidays at home. They were happy to be back in school, they said, which I hoped meant the coming days would be productive.

January's weather turned cold after the snow, and Johnny was still wearing the suede jacket with the fringe that he had gotten when Annabelle got her shoes. It was very precious to him, but it had only a thin lining, so I brought in a warmer coat with some other clothing I had been given. Johnny refused to take the warmer jacket. I could see his mental heels digging into the ground. He could not be convinced he would be better off with the warm jacket than with his magic one, so we finally compromised and added two sweaters under the jacket. He was still a man of the West. If confidence came with that fringed jacket, he needed it until he could build his own confidence.

Most of the class settled down during the first week of the new school year, but Donald continued to agitate. He practiced very little self-control and was as difficult to handle as he had been when he first came to the classroom. He made it almost impossible for the others to ignore him, with his habit of teasing, shoving, and poking others. The children went back to their former practice of giving him a wide berth.

The end of January brought report card time, a time of anxiety. Most of the children had picked up their peers' or siblings' concerns about grades or "passing." Getting good grades was much more important to them than what they had learned. I told them the marks weren't important, but the learning was, because it would be theirs forever. They looked at me with the old stoic look of doubt on their faces. Their experience had not taught them that.

The children were graded in comparison to their ability and the effort they had expended to learn. It was satisfying to me to be able to give good grades to almost all of them. I included notes to all of the parents, explaining my grading system and asking them to come to see me any day, before or after school. I hoped to talk to them about what their child was doing and what would help him or her achieve the most. Since I knew William's mother was working, I had been sending her notes regularly so she would know William was doing well and could be pleased with his progress.

Johnny's mother came to see me the following week. She was almost as shy as Johnny was, but she managed to convey her concern for him and her pleasure that he was making progress. She said Johnny loved school now and talked about his class all the time.

It was a pleasant visit, and I was happy to be able to tell her Johnny was well behaved and trying hard to learn. I was able to suggest that she ask Johnny's older brother to play ball with him occasionally to improve his coordination, and perhaps to read with him sometimes. His brother was fourteen, old enough to help, and was in a regular classroom, so I knew he must be able to read better than Johnny did.

Except for Nellie's mother, whom I saw at least once a week, Johnny's mother was the only other parent who came to see me. I was disappointed because I had hoped some of the other mothers or fathers would come. By working together, we might have been able to help the children more effectively.

The first of February brought Nora's birthday. The day before, we made birthday cards for her and planned to have her party after recess the next afternoon. Nora spent the morning wondering whether or not there really would be a birthday party for her. Although by now we had had several parties, each child still was surprised when we really had a party just for him or her.

At last, after recess, the time came for singing and eating ice cream and cake. Nora's smile became expectant, and she looked as though she were afraid to breathe as she opened the package that was a gift from all of us. It was a baby doll, so Nora would have something to love that was all her own. She was so obviously pleased that we all sat quietly while she examined the doll minutely, much as a mother would examine a newborn baby. No new mother could look more contented than Nora did.

Suddenly, Donald jumped up and grabbed the doll. He held it under one arm and gave the head a vicious tug, yanking it off the body. It was a sickening moment. The children were as shocked as when their neighbor had been killed. They didn't even "ooo-oooh"; they just sat and looked at Donald as if he were a monster. Even Donald looked uneasy with the silence of his classmates. Their expressions shut him out.

"It was just a dumb doll," he said defiantly to the room at large and then sat down.

When I went over and put out my hands for the head and the body, he slammed them into my hands with no argument.

Tears were running down Nora's woebegone face. The children looked from Donald to Nora. I reassured Nora that I would fix the doll that night. She gave me a forlorn little smile. It said she had been right all along, there would be no birthday surprise for her. I knew if I couldn't fix the doll after school, I could at least replace it that night. There would be a doll for Nora before school started the next day.

The closing bell rang, and I walked the children to the door. Donald must have expected me to keep him after the others left, because he walked last instead of trying to push to the front of the line as he usually did. When I asked him why he had done something to make Nora feel so badly, he said, "I din get nothin'."

I hoped it wasn't my imagination that made me think he looked a little bit ashamed of his actions. If he was, it was the first time he had really shown any awareness of someone else's feelings.

"Haven't I promised that you all will have birthday parties?" I asked. "Yours will be on your birthday in May, and you will get a present then."

"Doan think I'll have one," he muttered, and looked up questioningly.

"You will have one, and the rest of the children who haven't had a party will have one, too," I said. "Would you want someone to ruin your party or your present?"

"No." He spoke almost in a whisper. "I din wanna break that ole doll, but I was mad cuz I din get nothin'."

"Donald, you're going to have to learn to stop hurting other people for your own sake as well as theirs. You won't be really happy as long as you are hurting others, and someday someone will hurt you back. You would rather have friends than have everybody mad at you, wouldn't you?"

He squirmed and frowned while I talked. Then out came the pixy smile that must have gotten him out of trouble many times before this.

"We could get her another dumb doll," he said.

The other children were almost out of sight, and I had to let him go home then—still not sure whether or not he realized the consequences of his actions. This would be another depressing incident to add to his anecdotal record. In December, when his behavior had shown some improvement, I had hoped I would soon be able to ignore his condemning record as a thing of the past. Each incident of this sort was a gloomy reminder of my failure to help him learn self-control, and a reminder of the life of strife that could be his in the future. I hoped to help him avoid following in Sam's footsteps.

The school was there to teach the children academic subjects, but it was obvious it needed to teach them how to get along in their world, also. Without some self-control, Donald would not survive long in the real world, and, worse still, he would hurt many of the people whose lives crossed his. Somehow, self-discipline had to be nurtured in him. It would do him no lasting good to be controlled by another.

The next day, the class came in without Donald. His tardiness had ended long ago, when he had found he could get no breakfast if he was late. It looked as though he was going to be absent again. Perhaps he was finally aware that he had done something he shouldn't have and was insecure about coming back to school to face his classmates and teacher.

Nora was delighted to find her doll fixed. The whole class inspected it to be sure it was all right. The children seemed to be almost as relieved as Nora to see the doll whole again.

The cereal and milk were being passed out when Donald peeked around the door frame. He waited to be acknowledged before coming into the room. The mischievous smile was there, but it seemed a little tentative. Surprisingly, he waited for a sign of welcome before entering. This timidity was certainly not part of his usual behavior pattern.

When I greeted him, Donald came in and went directly to Nora's desk. Poor Nora was bent over almost double to protect the doll in her lap. She didn't look up at him, as if looking at him would invite some dire act.

Donald whispered something to her and put three pennies on her desk. He had repaid her for hurting the doll. Then he hurried to his desk and asked with his customary brashness, "Time for breakfast, Teacher?" His smile was absolutely angelic now and firmly in place. He knew he had done something to atone for his actions. It was yet another beginning, a fragile moment of peace.

That evening, I answered my doorbell to find my kind neighbor waiting. I looked at him, however, with mixed emotions. He had come to give me circus tickets for my class, as he had done every year since I began teaching. While I appreciated his generosity, I dreaded the thought of taking my current class to a place that was packed with other children, and where the excitement level was sky-high even for the average child. I knew it would be another learning experience for them, but I hoped it wouldn't be another one for me.

We talked about the chance to go to a circus in class the next day. No one in the class had ever been to one. When I emphasized the need for perfect behavior in a place like the circus, they all assured me they could behave properly, of course.

Accordingly, we began a search for pictures of the proper animals. All of the children remembered the elephants and lions they had seen at the zoo. Clowns were drawn when it was time for art, since they seemed to have erased themselves from every magazine and book in the room. Donald was by far the best at drawing them, and they made a welcome change from his earlier drawing topics. For his recorded IQ, Donald did have a great many details in his drawings. His characters always had features most of the children missed, such as fingers and ears, and to my relief, he seemed to have forgotten some of the details he had added when he was first in this class.

Fortunately, I found another teacher with whom to share the expense of the bus, and all the usual permission slips came in on time. Verna was kept at home again, which was a blessing since it would be impossible to take anyone to the washroom at the circus with the hundreds of children crowded into the area.

The rest of the children were almost in a state of dehydration from being taken to the washroom so often by the time the bus arrived that afternoon. We boarded it and rode in stately decorum. The effect of having the older and larger class sharing the bus with us kept Donald peaceful and Debra quiet.

When we got off, it was into a sea of buses and children, and I kept repeating our bus number over and over to myself. We held together through the ticket-taking line and got to our seats with Debra attached to my leg like a cast and my one hand attached to Donald like a handcuff.

My five best angels, with Sheila in the middle directly in front of me, were seated first. The rest of us filed in behind them, with Johnny in the aisle seat in front and Nellie behind him. I released Donald only when he was seated on my right, the side farthest from the aisle. Debra viewed the whole circus from my lap.

It was delightful. Even Fred laughed out loud with his surprisingly deep voice at the antics of the clowns. The children handled the tension of the more exciting acts as well as any child there, and no one asked to go to the bathroom! I was proud of them; they were ready to take part in some of the activities of the big world.

The bus driver found us. I don't know how he did it in that mass of children's faces, but he pulled up in front of us as soon as we came out of the building. We didn't have to search for the bus at all. The trip home was far noisier than the trip to the circus, but everyone was happy and the time for real problems had past. We had days of new material for talking, thinking, drawing, and writing stored up now for future learning activities.

It was fortunate that we did, because intemperate weather kept us inside most days now. The sky stayed darkly sullen, spewing snow off and on, and rattling us with its icy wind. When the snow stopped, the clear days were frigid, much too cold for the children to go out to the playground.

The classroom smelled of damp clothes, chalk dust, and a faint odor of urine. Now, because we often had that period most disliked by both students and teachers called indoor recess, we had the smell of a gymnasium added to those other odors. Windows could only be left open a small crack because of the cold, and fresh air was hard to come by.

It is difficult to decide whether children or teachers dislike indoor recess the most. There is seldom enough physical activity during it to relieve the tensions of study and the students' desire for activity. It puts a strain on the teacher's imagination to satisfy the student's need for action, and a strain on the disposition of the child who is forced to remain inactive.

"Simon Says" and all the action games known to teachers were acted and re-enacted in our room as prolonged bad weather caused these periods to continue. The best game for the children was "I Spy," because it allowed for their wide range of capabilities. I could give Norman difficult clues to challenge his thinking ability, such as finding an object that I described by its function, while Nellie could find something in a certain color.

As the intermittently inclement weather continued, we began to rely on modeling clay to relieve tensions during recess time. It could be pounded and squeezed to one's full satisfaction, and it engaged the children's imagination. They tried making all of the animals we had seen at the zoo and circus, plus people, dolls, flowers, and cars.

The latter were Harvey's preference, since he had had an intimate acquaintanceship with one. After his accident, he had begun to notice all types of vehicles and the differences between them. Nice rectangular vans were the easiest to make with clay, and they added the topic of shapes to our period.

Donald preferred to make men, whom he could violently bash together until they fell apart. Fred liked making little people, too, but it required more imagination to recognize them as such. You could tell they were people, though, because Fred talked to them.

Debra made flowers. She spent recess period after recess period shaping minute petals and placing them around a circle of clay. Her new-found patience was inexhaustible and quite amazing.

It occurred to me that the children were quite similar to the modeling clay. If you worked with them patiently and for a sufficient amount of time, they could be shaped. Some results required more molding than others, and the person who did the shaping made a vast difference. It was a tremendous responsibility.

Intermittent days of cold but not frigid weather came and went. The children went out to recess more often. Now, when the rain forced them to spend their recess time inside, we spent the time constructing kites in preparation for the day when the weather would be favorable for flying them. Constructing delicate kites with the varied abilities and coordination skills in this classroom was quite an experience. It was fortunate that we had several kite kits, because a few met untimely catastrophes—a clear case of too many fingers in the kite.

The day we had been waiting for finally arrived. The air was dry, and the sun burnt through the haze, leaving only a few clouds with ragged coattails scampering across the sky. We did not wait for the regular recess period but instead received permission to have our recess early, and alone. There was plenty of room to run with the kites on the empty playground, and no one to get in our way.

The two kites that had survived the construction period debuted with all of their fragile splendor. The more gentle children were designated as having the first turns at flying them, to be sure they would feel the sensation caused by the wind lifting the kite as they ran with it.

The "pilot" held the kite in one hand and a length of attached string in the other. A co-pilot ran next to him holding the rest of the attached string as a precaution, in case the launch was successful and the pilot became so excited that he released the kite, string and all. Most of the other children felt they needed to run along, also, as a cheering squad to encourage greater team effort. We had enough exercise to make up for several indoor recesses.

Donald's turn came. He was not faint-hearted about running with the kite, as some of the others were, but released it too soon. The fickle wind, which lifted it from his hand, let it plummet to the ground, where it cracked on the asphalt.

Harvey, after two failures, got the second kite into the air. Released slowly, it soared in the wind, followed by the cheers of the children. Their spirits soared with the kite.

Each child, in turn, held the string controlling the kite until the bell rang for the rest of the classes to have their recess. We lingered to allow them to see us flying that airborne marvel, so they would know what wonderful things the "retard" class could produce. Then the kite was slowly reeled in and caught before it could hit the ground. It graced our classroom wall for the rest of the school year, out of hands reach but a reminder of one of our successes.

Running in the wind was invigorating; the successful flight of the kite was thrilling. But the envy of the other children was the headiest experience of all, a rare champagne for this class.

Airplanes, helicopters, and even space ships are flown by real people. So was our kite.

IX

SPRING CREEPS IN

Sunny days replaced more of the gray ones as we crept into April. The rains washed away the sooty snow, and the ground was blown dry by the wind. The smell of spring was in the air, damp but welcome. Harvey's birthday drew near.

Harvey announced without much coaxing that, above all other things, he wanted some real roller skates with wooden wheels for his birthday. These were found and wrapped, ready for the big event when an emergency at home kept me from going to school the morning of Harvey's birthday.

This was the first time I had missed school since I had taken over the class in October. I called into the office for a substitute teacher. I asked that she tell the class that I would be there after lunch and we would still have Harvey's birthday party. Somehow, my message didn't get through to the children.

When I arrived after the noon hour, the children were just coming in from the playground where all the classes were sent after they had eaten lunch. Some of the children looked tense. They had the same look they had had in the fall, like aged elves suffering yet another disappointment. Debra's eyebrows formed angry thunderclouds on her forehead. Even Harvey looked dispirited, thinking his treat was surely lost. The sight of the wrapped package on my desk encouraged him though, and his expression returned to its usual brightness.

Several of the children, speaking all at once, strove to tell me what had happened in the morning. Debra had cried when she saw the substitute instead of me and had refused to do any work. Donald had been so "bad" he had had to be sent to another classroom. Verna had had an accident on the floor, again. (I had thought those accidents were a thing of the past.) Fred had gotten under his desk. From Sheila's high-pitched voice, I knew she had been excited and voluble all morning. Altogether, I did not envy the substitute. She probably did not envy me either.

We managed to get a little math and reading taken care of, since I was sure there hadn't been much reading in the morning. Then, shortly before recess, we gave Harvey his cards and gift. No prize winner on a national television quiz show looked more excited at winning than Harvey looked when he opened his skates. He was able to try them on outside right away, since the recess bell rang right on cue.

We all went out to watch Harvey. He did quite well on the skates. There was a cement walk which ran parallel to the asphalt playground that he used to skate on. He balanced himself somewhat comically, at times, by windmilling his arms frantically, but that did not lessen his delight. He magnanimously offered to let the others try out his gift.

As usual, the unknown was frightening to most of the children, and they wouldn't consider trying the skates. When Johnny was asked, he shook his head. He didn't trust his ability. He had finally mastered the balance board, but he still couldn't do some things, such as skipping, as well as other children his age. His coordination had improved enough that he now played ball with the children on the playground, though. Whatever he was given to do, Johnny kept trying to do until he mastered it. He had not had any dramatic spurts of achievement as some of the others had, but he moved slowly and steadily forward. His accomplishments were only achieved after much repetition, but they were well worth the effort because, once Johnny did master something, whether it was academic or physical, it was his forever.

Although Sheila was tempted, Donald was the only one to take Harvey up on his offer. He put on the skates and did almost as well as Harvey did for awhile. We were all careful not to laugh at Donald's wilder antics at keeping his balance. No one wanted to bruise his tender ego and incur the wrath of Donald. He finally failed to maintain his equilibrium, fell, and became instantly angry.

"Dumb skates!" was followed by a few words that caused me to call a quick conference with him. His invectives had been frequent in the fall when he had first joined us, and again after the Christmas holidays; but for the last two months, he had been relatively quiet, and his unwanted vocabulary had seemingly been forgotten.

He had taught me well, though. I had not forgotten that his moods could come and go as quickly as summer showers. When he had come in after lunch, I had remembered to talk to him about Harvey's birthday. I had reminded him he would have a birthday party next month and a present of his own.

Anger at the uncooperative skates was Donald's only negative reaction for the day. He did not try to break the skates or damage them in any way, and we managed to get through the day without having him attack anyone or destroy anything. This was so important for this class because these children picked up and reacted to other children's moods even more quickly than did the average child. Harvey's infectious pleasure was not diminished by further outbursts from Donald.

While the children ate their ice cream and cake, I sat and and watched them. I marveled at how much they had grown in spirit, as well as in learning. Some of the children were doing so much better than they would have if less had been expected of them or if they had been continually confronted with indignation and criticism. In almost every way their behavior was greatly improved. There would still be rough spots ahead, but surely the most difficult of our struggles were over for the year. Now the challenge was to maintain the learning momentum until the last day of school.

A few mornings later, the children were very subdued when school began. They didn't share with me what they were thinking about, as had become the custom for most of them, and I didn't ask. Because of their uncomfortable silence, we had to rely on a contrived story about the coming of spring for our morning story.

When they began writing the story, it became impossible for Harvey to remain in his seat. He kept jumping up to go to the windows, there to look up and down the street that, a few feet away, paralleled our long window wall. Seeing nothing, he would return to his seat, just to jump up again after another minute and return to the window.

As much as I felt it was important for the children to be able to move around the room when necessary, this was clearly a bit too much, and seemed to be a ploy to avoid the hated writing paper. It was unnecessary, and it was distracting the other children. Finally, somewhat annoyed, I told him to sit down at his desk and stay there.

"Why do you keep going to the window?"

"The Devils is marchin' today, Teacher," Harvey said, "and they gonna march right down dis street."

The Devils were, and still are, a very large local gang active in the area. Some of their leaders' activities are still current news, and some of those leaders are in prison. They were the reason all the children had to be in or near their homes after school, since the gang virtually controlled the streets in the afternoon and at night. This condition worsened in direct proportion to weather improvement, and it was necessary for the children to be careful all day long during the summer. They didn't have the respite of protected school hours then.

The whole class was listening to our conversation now and looking apprehensive. I wondered how Harvey had known about the march and I suspected that at least a few of the others had known about it, too, because of their excessively quiet demeanor. I did not want to add to their distraction, though, by talking about the gang any more than what was necessary to relieve their anxiety.

"Harvey, they won't bother you, I'm sure. Some of them are your neighbors," I reassured him.

Harvey was quiet a minute. Then he gave me a serious look of concern. "But they might hurt you, Teacher." Another thoughtful pause followed, until his natural optimism came through and he smiled. "But me an Johnny'll take care of you, won't we, Johnny?"

Poor Johnny looked a little dubious about this, but then he squared his shoulders and nodded. A slow smile spread across his face, and he nodded more emphatically. "Yeah," he said, in his normal soft voice.

That day was the second anniversary of the killing of Martin Luther King. We were in an area where many buildings had been burned, people had been injured, and there had been a good deal of rioting. Riots still broke out sporadically in the city. Marches and other occasions that might cause an outbreak had to be taken quite seriously.

The news had reached the main school, too, because shortly after our conversation, a directive came from the main school telling us to close all windows and keep all shades pulled down. We spent the rest of the day without our cheerful sunshine and, worse still, without fresh air. Fresh air was still a necessary ingredient in our room.

If the march took place, it did not come our way, and it was not reported in the newspapers. We spent our usual day studying, without interruptions. The children were still subdued, though, when they left for home.

A day or two later, a solemn-faced visitor appeared who stood, arms crossed, watching us through the window of our door for what seemed to be an interminable time. When all of the children grew increasingly fidgety under his scrutiny, I gathered up my courage and headed for the door. As I did, our observer turned and left. Whether or not this appearance was connected to the gang's attempt at dominance, or just why else he would be watching us, I'll never know. He was not noticed looking in at any of the other classes, and none of the children knew who he was.

Kevin came to school in a very upset state the next day. His grandmother had had a heart attack. She was in the hospital, that frightening unknown place. This woman, who had cared for him so well, was the only one he had been able to count on in his life, and his whole support system was threatened. He spent most of the day gazing into some chasm, which he visualized as opening before him.

His mother came home to care for him and his sister. Fortunately, Daddy didn't come and was never heard of again in this room. The insecurity of having a different "momma," even though she was his real mother, shortened Kevin's attention span again. What progress we had made wavered and faded as survival worries pushed out thoughts of reading and math.

Even Sheila's nagging had no effect on Kevin. She was more gentle about her nagging than she had been, though. She, and the rest of the class, showed some compassion for

Kevin's unhappiness. Here was another example of one of life's problems that had no remedy in the classroom but directly affected the amount of learning achieved in it. If no communication had been developed with Kevin and his problems were unknown, a teacher would assume he was being sullen or lazy.

The weather became stable and the sun grew insistently stronger, encouraging the little marigold seedlings each of the children had started from seed. They had planted them in two flats, which were kept on our sunny windowsills. The flats were large enough for each child to have a short row of seedlings all his own.

Each child had drawn a shallow row in the dirt with a pencil point, had taken five seeds, and had placed them in his or her row. Then they had filtered a little dirt through their fingers to cover them. Popsicle sticks with their names on them marked their own special rows.

The children took turns each day watering these seeds with a fine-holed sprinkler until the seeds popped open in a few days and little stems with two tiny leaves emerged. The joy with which the seedlings were greeted was a thrill to see. Few things in life are more dependable than marigold seeds.

After the seedlings became sturdy little plants the children took spoons, and carefully, gently, transplanted the plants from the flats to flower pots they had decorated. Each child then had a pot of little plants to take home for Mother's Day. Fred's, of course, was called an early Father's Day present.

Spring Creeps In 137

On the days when everyone else forgot to water the seedlings, Verna reminded me about them. She would come up to me and whisper "flowers." All the other children had trouble believing there would be flowers on those little seedlings, but Verna took it on faith.

One day, when I was watching Verna tend her precious plants, she said, "Me grow flower." She turned and looked over her shoulder, as if to see if someone else had said that. Then she peeked up at me and whispered, "Some kids doan wanna talk alla time."

Those were the first sentences she had said all year. The only other sounds that had come from her were one word replies when she couldn't avoid answering a question. Verna even cried silently. Who could really know what her IQ was. She had been completely nonverbal when she was tested, and she was too shy or frightened for anyone to establish rapport with her immediately in order to have a valid testing situation. No one knew why she wouldn't talk. It was obvious, now, that it wasn't because she lacked comprehension or the ability to speak.

There are methods for measuring the IQ's of nonspeaking children, but with an excessively timid child, the validity of those measurements has to be questioned. Intelligence quotients are supposed to reflect the rate at which children learn, but the rate is not necessarily even. Sometimes, a door seems to open for a child, and their mental growth spurts through the opening. Perhaps Verna was only waiting for her door to open.

It was a happy occasion for both of us. Verna looked directly at me and smiled, as if we now shared a secret.

Verna obviously was more comfortable in her world, and she would begin to learn more now.

It was the type of precious moment that is a teacher's most important reward. Some satisfactions are so slow in coming that you think they'll never arrive, but they are all the more valuable after the long wait. I thought of all the advice I had been given about not getting emotionally involved with these children. It was apparent to me that nothing short of getting involved and caring for them would help some of them. It was not the complete answer to all learning problems, but it seemed that just being comfortable and secure in their classroom allowed their minds to open up to learning instead of remaining rigidly closed to ward off the fear of failure. They needed to be led to education, kept in a warm place like seedlings, and sprinkled with the chance to learn until they were ready to grow mentally.

The most important things some of the children needed to learn were that they themselves were doing well and that they were really persons of value. No teacher training classes taught you this. Seeing their perception of themselves improve, and the mushrooming effect it had on their development was a lesson no teacher got in college.

When I began teaching this class, it was necessary to decide what each child needed the most and what, in addition to academics, would help them all get ready for their future lives. They were laboring against so many obstacles. They were hobbled by poverty. Cold, discomfort, and sometimes hunger were their regular companions. A tradition of hardship kept them from complaining, though. This was what they expected of life.

In addition, they were in a neighborhood that had seen far better days, and had in it fewer children who were easy to teach by the old standard methods, so many teachers did not want to teach here. As a class, they were considered less interesting to teach than others, since they needed a greater amount of repetition. Any feelings of accomplishment for the teacher were difficult to attain and slower to arrive, so most certified teachers preferred to teach other classes where rewards come more quickly and more frequently. Consequently, these children were often left with substitute or untrained teachers.

The children with emotional or social problems, as well as those with learning disabilities, were lumped together in this class with mentally handicapped children. The emotionally handicapped child's inability to learn, though, can't be explained by intelligence, sensory, or health factors, and that child needs far different help than the mentally handicapped child does. The variety of problems, in a room with all the combined handicaps, made solving each individual problem more difficult. The teacher's time was juggled between one child and another.

The children's parents, sometimes struggling with problems of their own, frequently were unable to work with a teacher to provide support and backup learning at home. They often felt incapable of helping and insecure about coming to school for conferences. Sometimes, their only contact with the school was when they were forced to come to hear some bad news about their child, so they became alienated from the school. Sometimes they had disliked school themselves or had no conception of the value of schooling for their children and so did not encourage regular attendance.

Teachers, who had taught here many years and had had easier children to teach in the past, sometimes actually disliked the children. The resulting "put-downs" scarred the children's egos and created a cycle of despair. These teachers were more apt to recommend lively or disruptive children for intelligence testing since, if they scored poorly, they would be taken out of their classrooms. Children with siblings in EMH classes were more apt to be recommended for testing, also. Some teachers expected them to fail because they were in the same family with others who had "failed."

The teacher who had declared, "They're all stupid," was creating a self-fulfilling prophecy. The many children who had gone through her classroom, and similar ones, had learned something that should never be taught to a child in school or anywhere else. This type of teacher thought she never failed to teach; the children just failed to learn.

Moreover, there was a shortage of school psychologists. It often took so long to get an appointment to have a child tested that he or she lost educational time by being left in the EMH classroom, frequently being forced to learn at a slower pace than necessary for too long a time. Other children were left too long in the regular classroom, where they continued to fail and to lose all confidence in themselves.

My first view of this class had shown me a group of children who were, for the most part, inordinately timid or defensively hostile because they felt rejected and unable to succeed. Ensuring that each child learn as quickly as possible and that each child felt worthwhile, no matter what his rate of learning, were the most important factors in my thinking.

Children's thinking processes are vastly underrated. They understand that some of their classmates learn more quickly than others. They understand that it is frequently easier for them to learn one subject than another, while the reverse might be true for their classmate. They can handle these ideas. What they can't handle is rejection and being made to feel that they are unable to succeed even at their own pace. These children did not need any more ideas that would impede their learning than they already had.

Notice came that Norman's intelligence test would take place the following week. Norman was still taking tests in our classroom. Harvey and Nora were just beginning the first grade reader, and by this time, I was giving them and the children who were reading in the second grade readers simple, but frequent tests, too.

The tests were not given to tell me what the children had learned. I already knew that. The tests told the children they were able to take tests and succeed at them. The fear inspiring word "test" should cease to be so stressful to the children after taking so many of them. And no matter what they were told when the psychologist came, the children almost always knew those IQ tests were not really games. As one child said after being tested, "It wasn't really a game; it was *work!*" After all his practice tests, Norman managed to take his test in a fairly calm manner. He returned to the classroom with no visible signs of nervousness. Now we had to wait for the results.

The coming of May whispered that the school year would be coming to an end soon. I worried that we were not ready

142 *Retard*

for it yet, but we must have been close to ready, because Donald had his own birthday party at last, and the excitement he felt did not cause him to hassle anyone else. Indeed, he acted the part of a genial host, insisting on passing out the cake and ice cream to each child and to me, all by himself. He was so agreeable that the other children relented a little and talked to him. They managed to treat him as one of the group instead of shutting him out of their conversations.

He was able to enjoy the party and was delighted with the basketball we gave him. He became so magnanimous that he even told the other children they could play with it, too,—someday when he brought it back to school.

He made this offer after recess, during which they had watched him bounce the ball around the playground for fifteen minutes. Of course, he never did bring the ball back to school to share with the others; that was a gesture he wasn't ready to make.

He did talk about playing basketball with Tyrone after school so there was someone with whom he shared. I hoped he and Tyrone would become avid basketball players and use up their extra energy in a better way than they had been accustomed to.

One of the children in the intermediate EMH class moved away to another school district, and Fred could transfer to that room now. After discussing it with the principal, the other teacher and I transferred him on paper only. He was doing so much better. He would never be able to do all the things other children could, but he was using some of his abilities now. The end of the school year was approaching, and there was no need to make Fred adjust to yet another new teacher this year. He would be doing the same work in either room. He would remain with us until the end of the school year, sitting on his chair every day, never under the desk.

X

SIGNS OF GROWTH

Our class was requested to entertain the Parent Teachers Association during its final meeting of the year. We tried several songs and decided to sing Ray Steven's "Everything Is Beautiful." It is a lovely song with an easy melody, and many of the children had already learned most of the words he used for an introduction at their churches:

> Jesus loves the little children,
> All the little children of the world.
> They are yellow, black, and white.
> They are precious in his sight.
> Jesus loves the little children of the world.

The rest of the song did not seem to have too many words, at first, but as the days went by, learning the words and coaxing each child to sing took part of many afternoons.

Explaining the words and having them give examples of beautiful things and people helped them learn the song. It also increased their awareness of beauty around us and of the good qualities of their classmates. Nellie always smiled, they said. Norman helped them and he didn't "mess with" them. Debra and Sheila helped, too. Harvey was always fun to be with. Johnny was big, but he never hit people. Annabelle took care of her little sister. They really understood the words when they sang, "Everybody's beautiful, in his own way."

All too soon, the day to perform came. The children invited their parents to attend and I wrote notes to each of them also. We planned an "after the show" party for when we got back to our classroom.

The day before the performance, Donald had asked me to tell him how he could wash his shirt by himself. I gave him as easy an explanation as I could, wondering if he would really be the one to wash it. The question showed a surprisingly intuitive awareness. Nothing had been said to the children about their appearance, yet Donald had thought of it by himself.

On performance day, I saw that either Donald or his mother had washed his shirt. It was clean, and so was Donald. All of the children looked clean and bright for their debut, and each of them felt very important that day. It was a warm, sunny afternoon, but Johnny still wore his fringed jacket for confidence.

We walked over to the main building in an unusually solemn procession. Sheila and Debra were quiet. Even Donald and Harvey were subdued.

The meeting was to be held in an empty classroom. And it *was* almost empty. There were four women there, including Nellie's mother. Two of the other women were the officers of the P.T.A., and the fourth one was the school crossing guard, who had come in for a visit until she was needed after school. Except for Nellie's mother, none of the women were related to the children in our class.

The other children's mothers had not come. I had hoped to be able to talk to Kevin's mother and Nora's mother, in particular, and perhaps even with Donald's mother. The contact would have benefited the children. Obviously, some of the parents could not come because they worked, but it was disappointing that the ones who could have come weren't there for the children's sake. None of the children showed any concern that their parents weren't there, though. They seemed to take this small audience for granted. Since I was not too confident of the outcome of our production, I was only disappointed for the children.

Norman, as elder statesman, announced our song, and we began. That is, some of us began. Not a sound came from Verna, Annabelle, Nora, William, Fred, Kevin, Johnny, or Debra. They stood as if transfixed, as I smiled hopefully and made beckoning motions with my hands—all to no avail.

Some slight murmur came from Sheila, Norman, and Harvey. Nellie hummed her own song. But Donald sang. He filled the empty classroom with his singing. He sang the words clearly. His body swayed. His arms were extended toward the P.T.A. members. He was truly "on stage." None of the adults noticed that not much sound came from the rest of the class. Who was here to notice?

Donald carried the day. His success became everyone's success. The rest of the children didn't appear to notice they hadn't really sung, but they knew Donald sang well. The little party we had after our show was a happy one, even without parents, except for Nellie's mother, of course. Donald was more accepted by the class that day than he had ever been, including the day he had hosted his own birthday party. He had contributed to the whole class, in a way, and he was obviously happy and full of camaraderie. The result was a group of happy, relaxed children.

When the children left for home, Donald's performance was added to his anecdotal record. It was not terribly significant as far as classroom behavior was concerned, but it was reassuring to be able to praise something he had done, note his improved behavior following it, and add something positive to that record.

The words, "Everybody's beautiful, in his own way," echoed in my head. Donald had been beautiful that day. His behavior during our party indicated he could be companionable when he felt good about himself and didn't have to prove anything to anybody. Maybe some teacher, anxious to find a way to praise him and give him attention for positive reasons, as I had been anxious to do for so long, would read this record and make use of his ability to sing. Praise for his singing could help him feel comfortable enough to earn praise for other behavior.

Dentist day came. This was not a day to which either teachers of classes such as mine or the children looked forward. Some of the children in the school were to be sent to the dentist in a van, apparently provided by some government agency. The list of those who were to go had a few of my children's names on it. Among the names was Johnny's.

Johnny was kind, and Johnny was easy to get along with, but Johnny was *not* going to the dentist. He told me so, and he told me so; nothing would allay his fear. When the time came to go out and get into the van, he was still telling me so. In fact, he had his legs wound around his chair legs and a firm hold on the seat with his hands so I couldn't even lead him out.

The only other thing Johnny had ever been so stubborn about was his fringed jacket, so I lined up the other children and told Johnny that he might not be going to the dentist, but his jacket was going. I guess Johnny thought he might never see the jacket again, because he hurried after us and put the jacket on as he entered the van.

When the children came back from the dentist, Johnny was the first one in the door. He happily showed me the hole the dentist had left when he pulled a tooth. He was proud of going to the dentist and getting a bad tooth pulled out. He was still wearing his jacket, of course.

໒ ᓚ ɔ

William came to school the next day with bad news. He would have to move again. His mother had received an eviction notice that said the building they lived in was scheduled to be torn down.

There had been a fire in his building the night before. If the pattern for buildings slated to be demolished remained the same as it had been for years, more fires at night would follow until all the tenants were moved out. The fires encouraged the tenants to speed up their search for new living quarters.

Signs of Growth 149

William told us his mother had gone to look at an apartment that she had heard was available. It was in a different school district, and William was not happy about it. He hated to move again and to have to begin making friends in a new school.

No word had come from the office yet about a testing date for William and Debra. I clipped large notes to each of their files. The notes said retesting had been applied for and recommended that their new teacher follow up on the requests. Hopefully, my successor would be a file reader.

An old friend of mine came to town for a visit. She called me and, since she was only in town for two days, insisted that she come to school and take me out for lunch. It was our only chance for a visit.

The children had been told she was coming. They had been reminded to say hello and to look her in the eye. We found her waiting in the hallway as we walked to the children's lunch area.

As I greeted her and turned to introduce my class, I saw the children through her eyes. It was a tremendous shock. I had not seen Sheila's scar for months. Harvey looked so small for his age. Nora looked so frail; her skin was transparent. I checked quickly to see if Fred's nose was running. It wasn't.

They were not as beautiful through her eyes as they were through mine, but they did not look the same as they had looked in the fall, either. The dull, worn-down look was gone, and their heads were up. A few of their smiles were tentative, but they all smiled and looked straight at my friend. It was obvious they felt much better about themselves. Even seeing them through her eyes, I felt encouraged about their future lives.

~~~

Our final festive occasion occurred a few days later. It was our celebration of the end of a good school year for everyone and the beginning of their summer vacation. We planned a trip to a small nature museum, to be followed by a picnic.

It rained the night before the trip, making the morning air smell moist and welcoming. We had a newly washed world, gleaming with sunshine, to add to our pleasure.

I had made provisions to ensure no troubles would mar our day. A young teen-aged boy had joined us, to be Donald's special partner. My daughter came along to help me with the rest of the children and with the picnic lunch. (Nellie's mother had a doctor's appointment and was unable to come. Letting Nellie go on a trip without her was a vote of confidence from her mother.)

All of the children, including Debra, climbed happily aboard the bus. We drove to the rustic little museum, located in a quiet forest preserve. Donald only managed one poke at Johnny during the trip, and when I began the well-known refrain, "Be kind," Donald finished, "to each other." By now, he could recite the whole litany. At least it went in his ears and out his mouth.

Of all the small forest animals that were on display in the museum, the rabbits were the most appealing to the children. Their soft furry appearance evoked a gentleness that most of them had too few opportunities to express. Each child was permitted to pet a bunny, which was held by an attendant. They enjoyed seeing the squirrel, the one animal they knew from their own neighborhood, racing to make his cage revolve and the other small animals on display, but they returned again and again to pet the rabbits.

Outside, the nature trails through the forest held no magic for them. They did not enjoy the smell of the evergreens, the sound of crunching leaves underfoot, or the sun filtering through the leaves of trees. In fact, the forest made them nervous. Even having just seen the small forest animals, they were unconvinced that this unknown territory was not dangerous and that there would not be unknown scary animals in the woods. For some reason, the one animal they were certain was in the forest was the bear. Seeing the smaller animals in the nature museum had surprised them, but it hadn't convinced them that there weren't other more threatening animals.

When Donald detected that some of the children were frightened, he increased their fear by growling and grabbing at them. He had to be swung to the shoulders of my teen-aged helper, where he rode happily and harmlessly. It was another reward for the wrong behavior, but it benefited the whole class.

The tall trees along the trail brought no feeling of peacefulness to these children. They did not want to look for small footprints. They wanted out of this place. This world was too different for them to absorb quickly. It was unknown and it was scary. We quickly adjourned to the picnic area.

In the open sunshine of the picnic area, it was all right to talk about the woodland trails and the tall trees. They also enjoyed talking about the small animals and they would remember them. The trip exposed them to a world very different from anything they had known before, and it was a valuable learning experience.

We ate our lunch and talked of uncomplicated pleasures: sunshine, the smell of summer, the soft breeze that touched us, all the beautiful things that were outside. We even had a visit from a butterfly.

My daughter brought out her guitar. She played while we sang the few songs we knew. When she stopped, William became brave enough to ask me to take his picture while he held the guitar as if playing it. It was unusual for William to do anything to put himself in the spotlight, and I was happy to take the picture.

My helpers organized a few games—playing tag, tossing a ball, and running races. The relay races were the best with the varied capabilities of the children divided equally among the teams. New allegiances were built among the three teams contending for the title of winner. The competition didn't destroy our good spirits, because Donald's team won so he could afford to be expansive.

When Donald finally did become too excited and began pestering the others, he was hoisted onto teen-aged shoulders again. He was happy up there. He could look down on us and rule the world.

It was a happy, tranquil way to say good-bye to the school

year. The children boarded the bus with feelings of self-satisfaction and added companionship with their classmates.

When we got back to the classroom, there was a notice from the office on my desk. It stated that Norman's test results had been received. His IQ score was above the range for the EMH class, and he would be returned to the regular classroom. The transfer would be effective in September, since there was only a day and a half of school left this year, but he had a definite classroom assignment in the main building. What a wonderful way to end the day!

The next afternoon, we walked over to the main school. We went quietly down the hall to where Norman's new class would be, so it would seem a little bit familiar to him next year. Since he had come directly to the annex from his last school, he knew nothing about the main building except for the assembly hall.

When we got back to the classroom, we talked about the coming school year so that the children could get used to the idea of possible changes. Fred knew he would be going to the intermediate EMH classroom, of course, because we had talked about it ever since his birthday. I wasn't sure whether or not he understood, but he seemed to accept it. Changing classes should be easier for him in the fall for having known about it now.

The principal had asked me to prepare to teach a new class that would be opened in the fall, so I knew I wouldn't be there with them, although I didn't tell them so. Instead, we talked about "what if" to help them get accustomed to the idea of a new class or a new teacher. By fall, a different teacher would not be a drastic change for them. The long summer would make this year just a memory, hopefully a pleasant one. We also talked about how well each of them had done this year. I told them that, since they had learned so much this year, next year would be even better for them, now that they knew how to learn and how to get along with others. No matter who their teacher was or what class they were in, they were going to do well.

Debra informed the class that if I wasn't there in the fall, she wasn't coming to school at all, but her voice lacked assurance. She really was ready for new people and new experiences. The little girl with the "honky" teacher, the muttering, frowning little girl with the tongue of a buzz-saw was gone. In her chair was a happy child who loved to read and who was doing very well in school.

The whole conversational theme of change must have been unsettling for Donald, because he became disruptive while we were talking. Afterward, when the children were moving their chairs up near mine so I could read to them one last time, he managed to hit Johnny, his favorite target.

I stood immobilized as Johnny turned, grabbed Donald, and threw him to the floor. He sat on him; he did not hit him. The many months of being Donald's patsy had finally brought Johnny to use his size and weight to retaliate. He felt confident enough of himself to decide he no longer had to be someone's punching bag. The tussle had to be stopped, but a little self-defense on Johnny's part was long overdue. And he didn't even have his jacket on!

The minute he was asked to, Johnny got to his feet with his sheepish smile. I had to grab Donald, however. He jumped to his feet, too, the second he was free of Johnny's weight and headed directly for the door.

"I'm gonna get Tyrone, an' he gonna beat Johnny up," Donald yelled. Tears of frustration streamed down his cheeks. No one in this room had ever retaliated this way before. Probably very few retaliated elsewhere, because Donald selected his victims carefully.

Johnny looked less than comfortable at the thought of the bully, Tyrone, but he was reassured when I managed to hold onto Donald and get him seated next to me. I reminded Donald that he had hit Johnny first and told him he shouldn't have to run to Tyrone when someone else defended himself.

While Donald thought this over, I read to the class until it was almost time for the dismissal bell. Then, while the other children took their chairs back to their desks, I talked to Donald and Johnny. Somehow, the two boys managed an apology, Johnny smiling shyly, Donald with his pixy grin, but each really smiling at the other.

When the children were leaving the school for the day, I kept Donald back for the final time. During our many talks, his face had held expressions ranging from solid boredom to one of awareness and, finally, to an expression approaching caring. He was amazed when I didn't talk about the scuffle but instead praised him for apologizing. I told him he wouldn't want to bother others so much now that he knew how to behave and how to make friends. I hoped the sweet honey of praise would stick to his memory for a while and the pleasure of the memory would help him try to earn more praise in the future.

Donald had not shed his manipulative behavior completely or his need to control the other children. It seemed terribly difficult for him to give up those skills in which he excelled, even though they were negative skills that ultimately harmed him as much or more than they harmed others. They gained attention for him but they had to be replaced by positive skills for which he could gain positive attention. Although he still showed more instability than the others, as the months went by he had shown improvement, too. He had improved his learning skills, and demonstrated a little more self-control most of the time.

Sheila had, too. She almost never shrieked now. Her voice was more modulated, and her behavior less frantic. Most important, she evinced a greater desire to learn. Fred had not been under his desk for months and moved around almost as the other children did. His lurching walk was gone and his eyes had a new awareness in them. His father had been working on hygiene with him, and he was really a different boy.

The sweet taste of success had sugared Debra's tongue. She was so happy with all of her new achievements that she forgot to attack others and entered school each day as an efficient secretary does, immediately going to her desk to get out the necessary equipment for the day. She was still a bossy little girl, but in a much nicer way.

Norman was a little less solemn and a tiny bit more relaxed, although his outlook on life would always be more serious than the average child's. Success had freed him from some of his rigidity, and he talked to and played with the others more often.

William was much more outgoing socially. He had made real friends now, and even though he would be leaving them, he knew he was capable of making new friends. He felt added confidence from doing well in school, and he had the firm support of his mother to aid in his continued success. She would never be lured into keeping him out of school unnecessarily again.

Harvey had not lost his happy disposition, but he was calmer, less easily distracted, and less distracting in class. He worked diligently to overcome his handicaps. He had never had a lack of determination to succeed, but it had been weakened by his learning problems. Now there was a possible goal ahead that he could see and for which he could strive.

Nora and Kevin had made some progress but they were both still hampered by the emotional encumbrances they carried, and I marveled at their courage to continue trying. They were both terribly unhappy, but no one in the school could help them in their out of school lives. The best that could be done for them was to provide a peaceful accepting atmosphere during school hours, a place where they could aim for and achieve reasonable goals and be appreciated for their efforts and successes.

Johnny and Annabelle had plodded along slowly, but had achieved new strengths. Repetition was giving them a good foundation to build on, and what they had mastered had truly become theirs.

Verna had learned a few skills, mostly manual, as had Nellie. They both smiled now, and Nellie still hummed from her limited repertoire of tunes. It was a contented, happy sound.

※

The last morning, the children came to school only to get their report cards and to say good-bye for the summer.

Although I would teach a different class in the fall, I would be here, too, in spirit. I thought I would be able to visit with them, once in a while, and follow their progress. At the time, I didn't dream I would know so much about their future lives as I do now.

For the final time, I reminded them that they had done so well this year that the next school year would have to be a great one for them. Their spirits had strengthened in the determination to succeed.

The year ended on a happy note. Who can be unhappy when they know they are doing well and someone cares about them?

It had been a successful year for all of these special children, to some degree, and a very successful year for many of them; therefore, it had been a successful year for me.

XI

LAWS FOR THE EDUCATION
OF THE HANDICAPPED

The year after I taught this primary EMH class, the federal government began a breakfast program for needy children. It was a great blessing for children in many school areas, one of which was this one. Because of it, children were waiting at the school door early every morning.

Three years later, Public Law 94-142 was passed. This law mandated education for all handicapped children and required that all states participating in the program, and thereby being funded by the federal government, develop a plan that would assure all handicapped children "a free, appropriate public education." At the present time, all of the states, with the exception of New Mexico, participate in the program, and New Mexico has applied for admission to the program. The law has become known as the "Education for All Handicapped Children Act" or EHA.

The law was to be phased in over a four-year period. It required states to maximize equal opportunity for all handicapped children between the ages of three and twenty-one by September 1, 1980. No longer were children to be excluded from school because of their handicaps. No longer were there "unteachable" children. Any teacher who has worked with EMH children knows that, at the least, they can be trained to do the less difficult jobs, and some can do far more.

While researching for PL 94-142, Congress found that of eight million children who were identified as handicapped in the United States, more than half were not receiving an appropriate educational program. The special needs of the remaining half of the handicapped children were not being fully met, either. Also, one million children had been excluded from school.

The Association for Retarded Citizens of the United States (ARC) estimates that three percent of the population of all ages in this country is retarded, and the vast majority (about 70%), of this 6.1 million people are educable.

The cost of educating the handicapped is admittedly greater than educating the nonhandicapped, but the benefits are evident. The Pennsylvania Association for Retarded Children's (PARC) legal case against the State of Pennsylvania heralded the beginning of less discrimination against handicapped children. It decreed that "all mentally retarded persons are capable of benefiting from a program of education and training. The greatest number of retarded persons, given such education and training, are capable of achieving self-sufficiency." Obviously, it is less expensive to train retarded or mentally handicapped children to become self-sufficient than to deny them an appropriate education and then support them for the rest of their lives.

Laws for Education of the Handicapped

PL 94-142 is a funding law. No state is required to accept funding under it, but those who do must provide the services and protections mandated by the law. According to the law, participating school boards must place the handicapped child in the least restrictive classroom; by law, that child is not to be included in the mentally retarded category. Those included in the handicapped category can only be removed from the regular classroom if they can't achieve with the nonhandicapped to the maximum extent educationally appropriate. Assuring that children are educated in the least restrictive environment has become known as the "mainstreaming principle." It allows borderline handicapped children to remain with their peers who are achieving at approximately the same rate of speed. At the same time, it recognizes that each child has different needs and attempts to answer those needs with individualized help.

That, in a way, is what was done with Norman. He was capable of achieving with his peer group and benefited from his association with it. For him, it made the transition back to the regular classroom much easier and gave him the confidence that being inappropriately placed in a special education class had shaken.

One problem that evolved from the principle of keeping students with their peers in regular classrooms is that some school districts that attempted to lower class sizes for groups of borderline students found there was no federal funding available to help them do so. Some districts that tried to have special classes for slower learners had to disband them because of lack of educational funds.

To be classified as mentally retarded under PL 94-142, a child must be subaverage in general intellectual function as measured by standard intelligence tests administered in the child's native language and, *concurrently,* the child must show deficits in adaptive behavior; that is, he or she must show less effectiveness in meeting the standards of personal independence and social responsibility expected of the same age and cultural group. Tests given to the children should include those that assess areas of educational need, not just those that yield an intelligence quotient.

Court cases across the country have accused intelligence tests of being biased measures when used exclusively to place minority students in special education classrooms. Inability to use standard English, differing cultural backgrounds, plus varying levels of communication skills all weighed heavily against the minority child when taking a standard IQ test. Courts and researchers found that black and other minority groups, such as Indians and Hispanics, occupied a disproportionate number of seats in special education classrooms. Even allowing for the deprived home conditions of some of these children, the percentage was too high. It was found that single test scores had often been used to determine placement in those special education classes. A single recommendation had often put the child in the testing situation in the first place.

Better evaluation methods and the use of additional criteria should modify this problem, however. If concurrent intellectual and behavioral deficits, as mentioned in the law are present, they must be manifest during the child's developmental period. And, "if a child can function in a regular classroom, that child cannot be included in a mentally retarded category," according to the law. Thus, this law has reduced the chances of misplacing children in EMH classes.

Instead of using only the intelligence quotient score for placement of a child in a mentally handicapped class, the law now requires that a multidisciplinary team be used for evaluation. The team consists of a psychologist, a social worker, a representative of the special education department, and the parents of the child. Medical tests are used, including hearing and vision tests. In many states there are local guidelines with additional requirements for evaluating and labeling. The evaluation obtained is then used to develop an individualized educational program (I.E.P.) for the child.

The I.E.P. is a written program that must be revised annually. Children's parents must participate at this meeting for revision as well as at the initial placement meeting, and all records must be available to the team. Parent participation is therefore fostered, and parents can no longer remain inaccessible to teachers and school personnel. By the same token, teachers and other school personnel must be accessible to the parent. Valuable communication benefiting the child results from the meeting of parents and school personnel.

The I.E.P. must be developed before the child is placed in the special education program. It must include statements of:

1. the child's present level of educational performance;

2. specific, precise educational and related services to be provided, and the extent to which children will participate in regular educational programs;

3. annual goals and short term objectives;

4. projected dates for beginning services, and the anticipated duration of those services;

5. appropriate objective criteria and evaluation procedures to schedule for determining, on at least an annual basis, whether or not short-term objectives are being achieved.

Since children in special education classes were often dismissed or disbursed to other classrooms when the special education teacher was absent, the law was recommended that a pool of substitute teachers, trained in EMH methods or interested in special education, be formed. However, there is still a shortage of special education teachers, school psychologists, and related personnel in some areas.

Teacher "burn-out" is more prevalent in some special education areas than in other teaching fields, and this attrition rate increases the shortage. While support systems for resource teachers vary from state to state and from district to district, they have improved since the new laws have been enacted and that should make the special education field more attractive to teachers. Many systems also have instructional aides who work on specific learning programs under the supervision of the teacher.

Various methods are being considered to reward teachers who spend extra hours developing I.E.P.'s or who add handicapped children to their regular class ("mainstreaming"). Additional compensation and/or released time to compensate for additional hours spent developing I.E.P.'s for the handicapped are being sought for teachers. The incentive of reducing the class size when mentally retarded are added to the regular classroom has also been recommended. More consideration should be given to class reduction, since that could help prevent teacher "burn-out" and the subsequent premature loss of valuable teachers.

Teachers who stagnate after teaching the same class year after year should receive consideration also. They need additional stimulus to help them remain interested in their students. Refresher courses or seminars might be provided every few years as they are in some states for regular classroom teachers. These courses would provide teachers with up-to-date knowledge and the added satisfaction that accompanies knowing they are keeping abreast of new methods for teaching handicapped children.

The Rehabilitation Act of 1973, PL 93-112, is an antidiscrimination or civil rights law that has also benefited the handicapped. Section 504 of this law prohibits discrimination against qualified handicapped persons in programs receiving federal assistance. "Non-compliance" violates a civil rights act and could jeopardize all federal funds to a state or local community, not just those funds connected to special education.

Section 504 of this law contains almost the same requirements for education as does PL 94-142. The law is enforced by the Federal Office of Civil Rights, however, and noncompliance can be more severely penalized. The law is therefore very important to the handicapped.

Former President Ronald Reagan, upon taking office, vowed to get the government off the backs of the people. He sought to eliminate unnecessary federal regulations, and to this purpose, he asked then Vice President George Bush to head a task force to study the problem.

One of the first laws reviewed by the committee was Section 504. As a result of the review, the Justice Department proposed amending the Section 504 regulations, an action that would have weakened the law and left the educational gains of the handicapped more vulnerable.

In 1982, the Department of Education also proposed changes in PL 94-142 that would have cut back on the services to the handicapped. The Select Education Subcommittee of the House Education and Labor Committee adopted a resolution disapproving the proposal. A national outcry from people and organizations across the country on behalf of the handicapped was heard in Washington. In November 1983, the Justice Department announced that it would not offer any new proposals relating to the educational laws. The Reagan administration announced that it was dropping plans to narrow Section 504, so the laws remained intact.

Responding to public opinion, President Reagan declared 1983-1993 to be the "Decade of Disabled Persons." The United States Department of Health and Human Services has funded the National Information Service for Health Related Services (NIS) for two years. NIS provides a free 800 telephone number for information on services for disabled children. The President's Committee on Mental Retardation is currently addressing the rights of retarded persons. It is also sponsoring activities concerned with the prevention of mental retardation.

The Education of the Handicapped Act of 1986 extends the reach of the Education for all Handicapped Children Act

Laws for Education of the Handicapped

(EHA) to disabled infants and toddlers. It requires that a written individualized family service plan, developed by a multidisciplinary team, be provided to the family of a handicapped infant. It recognizes that early identification and treatment of the handicapped is vital to their optimum growth and development. Encouraged by special incentive grants for the establishment of pre-school programs for three to five year olds, many states are now moving to include these children in the training programs.

While court cases continue to clarify the educational laws, and amendments continue to be added, the number of special education students has increased. In the most recent count, the 1985-86 school year, 4.4 million children receive special education; despite the declining enrollment in public schools. About eleven percent of the nation's school children receive some special education according to a study prepared for the government by Decision Resources Corporation.

Thirty-six percent of special education students are learning disabled, according to a count in 1981. The learning disabled group is now the fastest growing special education group, and it is clearly considered a separate group from the mentally handicapped. The growing number of learning disabled is primarily the result of new techniques that can identify learning disabilities, which in the past resulted in the child being labeled mentally retarded or emotionally disturbed. Indeed, learning disabilities can often lead to emotional problems if they are not detected.

Learning Disability "means a disorder in one or more of the basic psychological processes involved in understanding or in using language, spoken or written, which may manifest itself in an imperfect ability to listen, think, speak, read, write, spell, or to do mathematical calculations. The term does not include children who have learning problems which are primarily the result of visual, hearing or motor handicaps, of mental retardation, of emotional disturbance or of environmental, cultural, or economic disadvantage," according to PL 94-142 (EHA).

Clearly, many children who had learning disabilities were placed in EMH classes in the past, since placement was based on an average of the subscores on an IQ test. Although this average quotient might appear to be in the retarded range, a close look at the subtotals for a learning disabled child would show strengths in some areas and weaknesses in other areas. Therefore, children such as Harvey, Nora, and possibly others were labeled mentally handicapped instead of learning disabled. They consequently did not get all the help they needed. Techniques for teaching learning disabled were only beginning to be developed then, and few methods were known even to teaching staffs at universities.

Children with *severe* emotional problems, as well as *severely* learning disabled children, are now educated in separate classrooms when necessary. In this manner, the needs of each group of children can be met more freely and effectively. Schools are being encouraged to keep children with less severe learning disabilities or emotional problems in the regular classroom for the major part of the day ("mainstreaming"). The children then receive supplementary aid or tutoring for part of the day. This method enables the children to develop their abilities without isolating them from their peers. This is the least restrictive environment, (LRE).

Laws for Education of the Handicapped 169

Federal law requires that "to the maximum extent appropriate, handicapped children, including children in public or private institutions or other care facilities, are educated with children who are not handicapped, and that special classes, separate schooling, or other removal of handicapped children from the regular educational environment occurs only when the nature or severity of the handicap is such that education in regular classes with the use of supplementary aids and services cannot be achieved satisfactorily (Title 20)."

A study by the National Center for State Courts found that since 1976 almost fifty percent of the civil cases relating to education that were filed in state courts dealt with the rights of the handicapped. One of the most significant cases was the Rowley v. Hendrick Hudson School District case. In 1982, the United States Supreme Court reversed a lower court and the Second Circuit Court of Appeals in that case by finding that while EHA entitled handicapped children to a free appropriate public education, it did not guarantee a particular level of education. The court commented, "When that 'mainstreaming' preference of the Act has been met and a child is being educated in the regular classrooms of the public school system, the system itself monitors the educational progress of the child."

In 1983, the Sixth Circuit Court of Appeals, in the Ronacker v. Walter case, stated that EHA does not demand mainstreaming in every case but the requirement that it be provided "to the maximum extent appropriate indicates a very strong congressional preference." The least restrictive environment must always be considered.

Although PL 94-142 has never been funded to the extent originally intended by Congress, the law is clearly beneficial to all handicapped children. Hopefully, it reflects continuing social attitudes, because implementation of the new legislation is dependent on the attitudes of all teachers and parents. The interaction of more knowledgeable parents and teachers, who both participate in the development of the child's I.E.P. will provide a program that will help a handicapped child succeed. Helping the handicapped become more useful and their lives more meaningful through the implementation of these laws will benefit all of our society.

XII

PARENTAL AID

Parents of handicapped children frequently have been the resource least used by the school to benefit the children. But parents are the very people who have knowledge about their children that no one else has available. They know all of the conditions of the child's birth, early health problems, and early developmental signs, plus they are in a position to see current problems that might not show up in school.

Parents also have a vested interest in their children's development. Through their involvement in developing an individualized educational program (I.E.P), they help the child reach his or her potential. There are other ways for them to help, too. In addition to the I.E.P. meetings parents are required to attend, there are other meetings that relate to a child's education, such as school board meetings, PTA meetings, and parent-teacher conferences.

Visiting the child's classroom is a valuable aid to a parent. It shows the parent how the teacher is attempting to instruct the child, how the child responds, and the amount of participation the child has in classroom activities. Knowing what the school is currently teaching the child enables the parent to reinforce this learning at home and to evaluate the progress the child is making.

Discussing the events of the school day with a child is also important. It indicates the parent's interest in the school, and it helps the child develop communication skills. Talking with the child, telling stories, and reading books also help develop listening skills.

Parents should discuss with the teacher any problem the child is having. Even if the problem is occurring in school, the teacher may be unaware of it. If the problem is outside the school, it might give the teacher needed insight to the child's reactions in school.

Getting to know parents of other handicapped children also helps the parent. Such associations can sometimes lead the parent to local parents of handicapped groups or large organizations that work to achieve benefits for the handicapped, such as the Association for Retarded Citizens (ARC). Even if these parents are not part of any such group, they can still exchange information with the parent and provide moral support.

Parents who have just found out their child is handicapped need this moral support. They often have difficulty accepting their child's handicap and continue to hope a mistake has been made. Sometimes, they have ignored early indications that the child is handicapped to ease their own minds and fears. They sometimes react with embarrassment or project blame for the child's condition onto something or somebody else. Talking to other parents of handicapped children can ease these negative feelings and help parents move on to a position of helping the child. The earlier the child is helped, the fewer the emotional problems he or she will develop due to the handicap.

Sometimes educators can help parents learn to help their child by showing them how to adjust some of their child-rearing practices to benefit the child more fully. This instruction can take place through informal discussion groups, workshops demonstrating instructional activities to be done at home, or by helping parents form support groups. By receiving the encouragement and support of educators, parents can feel more comfortable trying different methods of handling their children, of promoting self-esteem, and of promoting self-discipline. Sometimes adequate nutritional or special diet information should be brought to the attention of the parent. All these benefits for the child can be more easily accomplished when the parents feel the personnel in the school respects and supports them.

It is important for educators to remember that, as a nation, we are made up of diverse cultures all deserving of respect. Teachers need to understand the home backgrounds of their students. When the teacher understands the home background and recognizes the individual differences among families, the teacher is better able to help parents deal more effectively with their children. Teacher training in parent involvement is often very helpful. Such training can be made available through in-service meetings or through college courses.

Home and school environments are sometimes quite different, but the parent who is made to feel comfortable in the school environment is more apt to take an active part in a child's education. When a parent comes to the school for any reason, it shows the child that school is important. Parent interest provides support for the teacher, also. When parents are involved, students achieve more.

In an article in *Education* the former United States Secretary of Education, William J. Bennett, stated that we need to foster and develop children's ability and motivation to take advantage of educational opportunity. He also authorized the publication by the U.S. Department of Education of the booklet *What Works* containing the following scientifically supported facts about learning. These apply to nonhandicapped and handicapped children as well. Some of the facts he listed are:

1. Parents are their children's first and most influential teachers.

2. The best way for parents to help their children become better readers is to read to them—even when they are very young. Children benefit most from reading aloud when they discuss stories, learn to identify letters and words, and talk about the meaning of words.

3. Children improve their reading ability by reading a lot. Reading achievement is directly related to the amount of reading children do in school and outside.

4. A good way to teach children simple arithmetic is to build on their informal knowledge. This is why learning to count everyday objects is an effective basis for early arithmetic lessons.

5. Children who are encouraged to draw and scribble "stories" at an early age will later learn to compose more easily, more effectively, and with greater confi-

dence than children who do not have this encouragement.

6. A good foundation in speaking and listening helps children become better readers.

7. Many highly successful individuals have above-average but not extraordinary intelligence. Accomplishment in a particular activity is often more dependent upon hard work and self-discipline than on innate ability.

8. Belief in the value of hard work, the importance of personal responsibility, and the importance of education itself contributes to greater success in school.

9. Parental involvement helps children learn more effectively. Teachers who are successful at involving parents in their children's schoolwork are successful because they work at it.

10. Children get a better start in reading if they are taught phonics. Learning phonics helps them to understand the relationship between letters and sounds and to "break the code" that links the words they hear with the words they see in print.

11. Children get more out of a reading assignment when the teacher precedes the lesson with background information and follows it with discussion.

12. Children learn science best when they are able to do experiments, so they can witness "science in action."

13. Telling young children stories can motivate them to read. Storytelling also introduces them to cultural values and literary traditions before they can read, write, and talk about stories by themselves.

14. Children in early grades learn mathematics more effectively when they use physical objects in their lessons.

15. Although students need to learn how to find exact answers to arithmetic problems, good math students also learn the helpful skill of estimating answers.

16. Teachers who set and communicate high expectations to all their students obtain greater academic performance from those students than teachers who set low expectations.

17. Children's understanding of the relationship between being smart and hard work changes as they grow.

18. Constructive feedback from teachers, including deserved praise and specific suggestions, helps students learn, as well as develop positive self-esteem.

19. Students tutoring other students can lead to improved academic achievement for both student and tutor, and to positive attitudes toward coursework.

20. Frequent and systematic monitoring of students' progress helps students, parents, teachers, administrators, and policymakers identify strengths and weaknesses in learning and instruction.

21. Schools contribute to their students' academic achievement by establishing, communicating, and enforcing fair and consistent discipline policies.

22. How much time students are actively engaged in learning contributes strongly to their achievement.

23. When teachers explain exactly what students are expected to learn, and demonstrate the steps needed to accomplish a particular academic task, students learn more.

24. The ways in which children study influence strongly how much they learn. Teachers often can help children develop better study skills.

25. The most important characteristics of effective schools are strong instructional leadership, a safe and orderly climate, school-wide emphasis on basic skills, high teacher expectations for student achievement, and continuous assessment of pupil progress.

These principles apply in varying degrees to handicapped children as well as to the average and above average student. Although the needs of the handicapped student are sometimes different from those of the regular student, they are more often the same. The above list should be considered by the parent as well as by the teacher when I.E.P.'s are written. Certainly, there is much room for raising the expectations for learning in handicapped children, and the principles listed can provide a guide.

Another source of information for the parent of a handicapped child is the Director of the Department of Special

Education for the state. This department should maintain a wide range of information of value for parents. Parents who write to the director in their state capital can obtain a list of booklets and materials available. The materials usually cost very little.

Among the excellent state publications for parents of the handicapped are two booklets published by the Wisconsin State Department of Public Instruction, Division for Handicapped Children and Public Services, in Madison, Wisconsin. The booklets are titled *An Invitation to Play* (nos. 1 & 2). They contain a teacher's guide for parents to encourage them to play with young handicapped children. They describe the levels at which children play, the social stages of children, ways of enhancing play, and how to observe play. There are suggestions for activities and the use of "throwaways" as resources. This type of appropriate play helps the child learn.

The EEN Triangle of Support: A Guide for Parents was also published by the Wisconsin Department of Public Instruction in 1987. It is a comprehensive guide. The Teachers College Press, in New York City publishes *The Special Education Handbook: A Comprehensive Guide for Parents and Educators*, by K. Shore. The State of New Jersey publishes *Special Rights for Special Children*. It is a manual for the parents of handicapped children in New Jersey. *Special Education: Parents and Students Rights* is published by the Texas Education Agency, Division of Special Education, in Austin, Texas. It describes the rights of the handicapped in Texas and the agencies providing assistance.

Nationally, the United States Department of Education, Office of Education, Research, and Improvement, publishes a booklet concerning the extension of the school year for the handicapped. Year-round schooling would eliminate regression over the summer and the time lost relearning skills. Instead of losing those skills, continuous application would reinforce them.

There is also a list of available publications involving the handicapped that is published by the federal government. It can be obtained by writing the Superintendent of Documents, United States Printing Office, Washington, D.C.

Schools can and sometimes do bring this type of information to the attention of the parent. Some school districts also provide a parent coordinator who explains procedures to the parent, answers questions, and can lead the parent to further information.

All parents have the right to information and records concerning their child. As stated, they can contribute in writing the child's I.E.P. If they are not satisfied with the program the school provides, there are four steps a parent can take in this order:

1. Discuss the problem with the school.

2. Ask for a "due process" hearing (due process means the right to be treated fairly).

3. Appeal to the state superintendent of schools.

4. Take the matter to court.

Recently, a law that allows parents to "prevail" was enacted. "Prevailing" means that the educational agency must make a change in the child's educational program as a result of the parents' action. This law was considered necessary because, in July 1984, the United States Supreme Court ruled in *Smith v. Robinson* that, when an individual's rights are covered under PL 94-142, they have no protection or legal course of action under Section 504 of the Vocational Rehabilitation Act or under any other civil rights statutes.

Under PL 94-142, there was no legal authorization for the courts to award parents who prevailed in court any reimbursement for the costs they incurred while pursuing the proceedings. Before the Supreme Court ruling, parents going to court sued under both laws, and attorney fees were reimbursable under Section 504. When the court eliminated Section 504 as a course of action in *Smith v. Robinson,* there was no longer any authority for courts to award payments of fees, even when parents did prevail.

In response, PL 99-372, called the Handicapped Children's Protection Act of 1986, was enacted. This law authorizes reimbursement of attorneys' fees to parents who prevail in administrative proceedings or court hearings. The statutory rights repealed by the *Smith v. Robinson* decision were restored by providing that Section 504 and other statutes be re-established as concurrent but separate vehicles for ensuring the rights of handicapped children. Thus when parents "prevail," they may now be awarded reasonable fees for legal services and other expenses incurred in providing adequate representation.

Booklets are available to help parent advocacy under this law. *Educational Rights for Handicapped Children: A Parent Guide* can be obtained from the Children's Defense Fund, 122 C Street N.W., Washington, D.C., 20001. Help may also be obtained by writing the Division of Advocacy for the Developmentally Disabled, C N 850, Trenton, New Jersey, 08625.

In general, teachers are professionals and are well qualified to evaluate the needs and performance of children. Frequently, they can recommend programs that are most suitable for the child's development.

If, however, a parent does not feel that the placement or program for his or her child is the most beneficial, the parent, following the steps previously described, can request a hearing regarding the identification of the child's problem, the evaluation, placement, or educational program of the child. Parents have a right to see all of their child's records and to have an independent evaluation performed. If the school's program is deemed appropriate by an independent evaluation, the parent must pay for the independent evaluation. If it is found that the school's program was inappropriate, however, the school must pay for the costs at public expense.

Although schools are generally correct in placements of students, there can be errors and abuses. In a survey conducted for the Council of Great City Schools by Research for Better Schools of Philadelphia, the council found that many large city districts were referring greater numbers of children into special education programs. These school districts seem to be putting underachievers into special education programs. Special education, in other words, may be becoming a "catch-all" for children who are not doing well in school. Since it is sometimes difficult to differentiate between the learning disabled and the unmotivated student, the learning disabled classes are getting most of these at-risk students that the school system has not been able to reach.

Since district achievement test scores usually do not include test results from the special education classes, the possibility of misuse of the learning disabled category becomes greater as the pressure for accountability of educators increases. For example, removing a good number of the lowest reading scores will naturally raise the overall reading score of the grade being tested in any school district. Every parent should be alerted to the possibility of this practice. It is not a new practice, but hopefully it is a seldom used one.

In 1988, a U.S. administrative law judge ruled that Chicago's public schools discriminate against handicapped students by violating federal and state laws requiring that students be properly tested and provided with services. Chicago was the second school system in the country to be the target of fund elimination in 1988.

An investigation by the U.S. Department of Education revealed that some students referred for testing waited for 120 to 150 days for evaluation, well over the (state) maximum of 60 days. The investigation found that forty-one percent of the students needing special education were not given attention during the legal time limit. Some students waited up to two years for services, and as many as 5,000 students have been affected by the school system's delays.

Investigators also found that parents were not notified when their children were to be tested, were not asked for their written consent for services, and were not included in conferences to discuss their children. If parents are not alert to the circumstances of their child's education, the child may be misplaced or left in the wrong class long enough to suffer a frustrating loss in educational time.

To avoid any lack of motivation that puts a child in jeopardy as an underachiever and a possible target for misplacement, parents should work with the child to make sure he or she enjoys the feeling of accomplishment brought about by mastering the tasks appropriate for the child's age and ability. Their praise for the child's success will build self-esteem and foster a desire to attempt mastering subsequent skills.

If parents establish reasonable rules for the child to follow and enforce them consistently, the child will learn self-discipline. The confident, self-disciplined child can now be helped to establish realistic goals alone. This applies to the child who is handicapped as well as to all other children.

The child who has developed self-discipline and a positive self-image is unlikely to become an underachiever, unless unrealistic expectations are placed on him or her, or the school placement is incorrect for the child's stage of development. Continuing success is therefore dependent on accurate placement in school and on the correct instruction for the child.

PL 100-630, the Handicapped Programs Technical Amendments Act of 1988, amends EHA and provides continued funding for programs that benefit the handicapped. It also strengthens provisions for the training of personnel who work with the handicapped and "encourages" the participation of parents in the development and operation of programs.

When the new philosophy of educators and parents working together is adhered to, the handicapped child should benefit greatly. Higher expectations for achievement, when appropriate, added to increased awareness of the methods of attaining these achievements, should allow the handicapped child to realize most or all of his potential.

Epilogue

The years following my teaching this class were busy ones, but I managed to keep informed about the progress of most of my "annex children."

William had, of course, moved away. I did not hear of him again, but I thought that with his mother now fully involved in his education and with his own strengthened motivation, he would continue to succeed.

Norman, as planned, returned to the regular classroom in the main school. He was on the same floor as I was that next year, so I saw him regularly. He had an excellent teacher and continued to do well in school. He, too, transferred schools the following year, and I did not see him again, but I knew he would continue to progress steadily in the future. He was determined to succeed. My only regret for him was that life was such a serious thing, but perhaps that characteristic was what made him strive so diligently.

Debra was retested and reassigned to the regular classroom. She followed Norman to the main school and remained interested in reading. She was a happy, well-adjusted child.

Nora, much to my sorrow, was drowned the second summer after I taught her. She was just ten at the time. Although her future had looked anything but bright, it saddened me to know that her life was lost before she had an adequate chance to live it. When I saw the article in the newspaper about her death, I had an instant, vivid recollection of her tremulous smile and meek demeanor. Now, at least, she would have no more fears to confront, armed only with that smile.

Fred's father died the same summer Nora drowned. Since there were no other known relatives, the court placed Fred in a residential institution. It is possible that he received more attention there than he had at home. Even if it is at a slow pace, I hope he is still learning in his new home. And I hope he's sitting on his chair.

Except for Kevin, the other children remained in that primary EMH classroom in the following years, progressing to the intermediate EMH classroom at the age of ten. Kevin's grandmother had another heart attack—this time a fatal one. Apparently, his mother reclaimed him and his little sister and moved them to her home, because, when I asked in the office, I learned that his records had been transferred to another school.

Three years were to pass since we were together in that classroom before I would find out more about Kevin. Then, one day, he walked into my classroom and greeted me as if we had just parted the day before. He had come back for a visit. Actually, the number of students who came back to visit their old school always amazed me. Apparently, visiting a school where they were known and cared for gave them a feeling of continuity in their lives.

Kevin told me where he was living and the name of the school he was attending. Then, he pulled up his shirt and showed me a three or four inch scar on his abdomen.

"Teacher, I was sittin' in the house, watchin' the television an' my sister call me to come help her. Some boy from cross the way was messin' with her." Kevin looked indignant as he recounted his story.

"I went out an' I rassle him an' shove him away. Me an' Carrie went back in the house. I was sittin' watchin' the television again, an' I feel somethin' wet on the front of me. That was the firs' I know I ben stabbed. I din feel it, an' I din even see he have a knife."

Apparently, nothing vital was punctured, because the doctor told Kevin he was in good physical shape now. That was the last I knew of Kevin. He was an unhappy looking eleven-year-old at the time, just as he had been an unhappy looking eight-year-old at the end of our school year together. Although he was unhappy, he still remembered that he had to take care of his sister. Of course, he had had a dramatic lesson in child care, a lesson not easily forgotten.

At the end of that school year, four years after our annex class, I transferred to another school that was closer to my home. When I have the opportunity, I still go back to my old school to find out how my past students are faring.

Nellie's mother, with extra time on her hands, took a job in the school cafeteria, so I always have a good source of information about the neighborhood. As she had told me when we first met, she knows almost everyone around there.

Students of various ages have come and gone through my life. Many of their lives I have been able to follow, and several of my students have made a point of keeping in touch with me. No group of children as a whole, though, has haunted me as much as does the group of children from the annex EMH class. Perhaps it was their extreme vulnerability and the almost herculean effort they would need to make to develop to their fullest capacities that brings my thoughts back to them. Although not all of them used all of their capabilities, some of them undoubtedly did. In time, some of the rest of them might be encouraged to use their neglected abilities, too.

Some of the children were ultimately able to contribute to their associates and society in general. All of them were capable of doing so, in their own unique way.

After completing her schooling, Nellie began working in a sheltered workshop. She puts products in boxes as they come down a conveyer belt. She likes it very much there and enjoys the company of the other handicapped people with whom she works. She is said to be a steady worker and does not get bored with a job that many people would complain about. She is needed in our world, and she has found her place in it. I'll bet she still hums as she works.

When Harvey finished school, he went to work for the park district. Most of his time was spent working with children in after-school programs. He must have brought the children joy, since he always wanted everyone to be happy. He had a natural aptitude for making those around him feel better about everything.

Debra works in a hospital. She has a little girl of her own now who has two starched pigtails. I'm sure Debra never calls her little girl "bad" or "retard," as she and some of the others in her class were called. Her little girl shows the security only gained by receiving a lot of love and approval.

Johnny completed a work-study program. He has a job in the factory where he was first employed when he was still in school. He has been there for several years and he is a steady, dependable worker, just as he was steady and dependable as a boy. He is the same shy, kindly person he was at eight. I met him on the street outside of the main school the other day.

As we stood on the playground talking, it was easy to see why there are so few students left in this area now. The blocks on each side of us and the block facing the school have irregularly placed buildings on them with many empty spaces in between. Here and there you can see a cluster of old houses, gathered together like gossiping old women wearing sooty dark dresses, with their unpainted porches making dingy aprons for them. A few deserted houses look resentful at being abandoned and turn their boarded-up eyes inward. Perhaps they are lonesome for the sound of children's voices.

Since the school population has decreased drastically over the years, the annex has long been closed and its classes moved to the main school.

Johnny, too, has moved farther out in the city, but he still keeps in touch with some of his old neighbors. When I saw him, he was stopping by the school after work to get the latest neighborhood news, just as I was doing.

He told me Donald had gotten in trouble, and he thought he was in jail. He had seen Annabelle and Verna in church, but he didn't know what else they were doing with their lives. No one knows where Sheila is, or what has happened to her.

Johnny didn't have to tell me what had happened to Harvey. I had read about him in the newspaper the night before. It was almost April, near Harvey's birthday. I had been thinking about him as I often do around the first of April. Perhaps that's why his name seemed to jump out at me from the small article in the newspaper.

"Man Shot on Street Corner" was the heading. According to the article, Harvey was on his way home from work and he had stopped on the corner to talk to a friend. Someone fired a gun from a passing car—a gang-related type of action. Harvey was hit by one of the bullets.

The police were quoted in the paper as saying the shooting was just another case of mistaken identity. It was spring recruitment time for the gangs, and they were out to intimidate their rivals. Harvey was just at the wrong place at the wrong time, as happened too often in his life and the lives of his peers.

I thought of the lively boy who had wanted everyone to be happy. The same boy who, fearing the gang was coming, had said, "Me an Johnny'll take care of you, Teacher."

Happy birthday, Harvey. I hope they give you chicken, wherever you are.

BIBLIOGRAPHY

Bennet, William J. *Education* 108, No. 2 (Winter 1987).

Bennet, William J. *What Works.* U. S. Department of Education, 1986.

Clearinghouse Review. Vol. 20, No. 9 (January 1987).

Chavkin, Nancy, David L. Williams, Jr. "Critical Issues in Training for Parent Involvement." *Educational Horizons* 66, No. 2 (Winter 1988).

Council for Exceptional Children. *Handicapped Children's Protection Act, P. L. 99-372.* Reston, Virginia: Department of Governmental Relations.

Cremins, James J. *Legal and Political Issues in Special Education.* Springfield, Illinois: Charles C. Thomas, Publishers, 1983.

Goldberg, Steven S. *Special Education Law, A Guide for Parents, Advocates, and Educators.* New York: Plenum Press, 1982.

Griswold, Phillip A. *Parent Involvement in Unusually Successful Compensatory Education.* Portland, Oregon: Paper, Northwest Regional Educational Laboratory, 1986.

Hirsch, Elizabeth S. "Parent Attitude Change through Involvement: An Examination of the Dynamics That Can Facilitate Parent Growth in Preschool Settings." Paper presented at the World Organization for Early Childhood Education, Jerusalem, Israel, 1986.

Jones, Phillip R. *A Practical Guide to Federal Special Education Law.* New York: Holt, Rinehart & Winston, 1981.

Jowett, Sandra, and Mary Beginsky. "Parents and Education: A Survey of Their Involvement and a Discussion of Some of the Issues." *Educational Research,* 30 (February 1988).

Kotze, J. M. A. "Educational Aid to Parents of Young Handicapped Children." Paper presented in the Republic of South Africa, 1986.

Lange, Jenny, and Connie Zieker. *An Invitation to Play: Teachers Guide and Parent Booklet* No. 2. Wisconsin Department of Instruction, Division for Handicapped Children and Pupil Services, August, 1986.

Martin, Reed. *The Impact of Current Legal Action on Educating Handicapped Children.* Champaign, Illinois: Research Press, 1980.

"Mental and Physical Disability." *Legal Reporter* (January 1987).

New Jersey, State of. *Special Rights for Special Children, A Manual for Parents of Handicapped Children.*

Orsini, Bette S. "Changing Labels is Quick Route to Re form for Some Schools." *St. Petersburg Times* (September 1987).

Rapp, James A. *Education Law* Vol. 3. New York: Matthew Bender & Co., 1985.

Salomone, Rosemary C. *Equal Education Under Law.* New York: St. Martin's Press, 1986.

Scott-Jones, Diane. "Families as Educators: The Transition from Informal to Formal Learning." *Educational Horizons* 2 (1988).

Shore, K. *The Special Education Handbook: A Comprehensive Guide for Parents and Educators.* New York: Teachers College Press.

Shrybman, James A. *Due Process in Special Education.* Rockville, Maryland: Aspen Publication, 1982.

Stowitschek, Carole. *A Parents Guide to the Education of the Handicapped Child.* Bismarck, North Dakota: North Dakota State Department of Education.

Thomas, Karen M. "City Schools Found Biased Against Handicapped." *Chicago Tribune* (August 1988).

Thomas, Stephen B. *Interpreting the Education of the Handicapped Act.* National Agency on Legal Problems of Education, 1985.

Turnbull, Rutherford, III. *Legal Aspects of Educating the Developmentally Disabled.* National Organization of Legal Problems.

United States Congress. *Education for all Handicapped Act, PL 94-142.* 94th Congress. 6th Session 1975. S. Rept. 1401.

United States Congress. *Handicapped Programs Technical Amendments Act of 1988, PL 100-630.* 100th Congress, 2nd session, U. S. Code Congressional & Administration News, West Publishing Company, St. Paul, Minnesota, 1989.

Wisconsin Department of Public Instruction. *The EEN Triangle of Support: A Guide for Parents.* 1987.

Wolf, Judith M. "Another Step Toward Mainstreaming for All Children." *West Education Law Reporter* Vol. 1, 1985, p. 441.

Yearbook of School Law, National Organization on Legal Problems, 1986.